Criminal Justice
Recent Scholarship

Edited by
Marilyn McShane and Frank P. Williams III

A Series from LFB Scholarly

Police Information Sharing
All-Crimes Approach to Homeland Security

Ernest D. Scott Jr.

LFB Scholarly Publishing LLC
El Paso 2009

Library of Congress Cataloging-in-Publication Data

Scott, Ernest D., 1957-
  Police information sharing : all-crimes approach to homeland security /
Ernest D. Scott Jr.
    p. cm. -- (Criminal justice : recent scholarship)
  Includes bibliographical references and index.
  ISBN 978-1-59332-322-6 (alk. paper)
  1. Florida Integrated Network for Data Exchange and Retrieval. 2.
  Law enforcement--United States--Data processing. 3. Criminal
  investigation--United States--Data processing. 4. Information storage
  and retrieval systems--Criminal investigation. 5. Police communication
  systems--United States. 6. Criminal behavior, Prediction of. I. Title.
  HV7936.A8S355 2008
  363.2'3028557585--dc22

2008034682

ISBN 978-1-59332-322-6

Printed on acid-free 250-year-life paper.

Manufactured in the United States of America.

TABLE OF CONTENTS

v

LIST OF TABLES

LIST OF TABLES (continued)

LIST OF FIGURES

ACKNOWLEDGEMENTS

Many members of the criminal justice community have made important contributions to advancing the cause of police information sharing. Here, however inadequately, I gratefully acknowledge a few valued associates who have played critical roles in Florida's information sharing effort and who have supported the research reported in this book.

Orange County Sheriff Kevin Beary provided money, personnel, and (most importantly) political muscle as the initial "champion" of the FINDER project that is the focus of this research. He made certain that the post-9/11 need for police information sharing was understood in both Tallahassee and Washington.

Dr. K. Michael Reynolds, at the University of Central Florida, gave feet to the effort by envisioning and creating the Florida Law Enforcement Data Sharing Consortium. He built the bridge between police practitioners, academics, and technologists to make information sharing a reality. He provided crucial assistance to the research reported here and continues to guide research aimed at understanding and improving information sharing systems.

Captain Mike McKinley (former) and Master Deputy Jim McClure (current) Chairs of the Data Sharing Consortium – and both of the Orange County Sheriff's Office – must be credited with institutionalizing information sharing across Florida's police agencies. Their tireless work on behalf of the law enforcement community cannot be overstated. Both of them provided me time, data, and encouragement in my research efforts.

CHAPTER 1

Traffic Tickets & Terrorists: the Information Sharing Gap

Most Americans are familiar with the concept of the police using computers to "run a check" on the people they encounter. There is an attendant belief that this computer check looks into a mammoth database supported by detailed data contributions from the nation's policing jurisdictions. The reality, however, is that most police records are *not* shared between agencies. America's 18,000 politically autonomous law enforcement organizations tend to collect information in stand-alone records management systems that do not communicate with each other. Further, many smaller agencies may not have any automated information to share because they don't have computers to enable information collection (Reynolds, Griset, & Eaglin, 2005; Reynolds, Griset & Scott, 2006)

This absence of information sharing is particularly true of "low-level" information. This is information that is generated by routine police activities such as traffic stops, crime reports, administrative reports, calls for service, and miscellaneous contacts with people who are not arrested or who are charged with minor offenses (Carter, 2004; Reynolds et al, 2005, 2006). Indeed, the failure of U.S. law enforcement agencies to share low-level information from everyday police operations has been identified as a factor contributing to the 9/11 terrorists' ability to execute their crimes.

Four days after the September 11, 2001 attacks on the U.S., reports of an incident emerged that provided a dramatic example of the information sharing gap:

> On April 26, 2001, a sheriff in Broward County, Florida, stopped the vehicle of Mohamed Atta, one of the men responsible for the terrorist attacks of September 11, 2001. The sheriff issued Atta a ticket for driving without a license and ordered him to appear in court. Authorities in Broward County never had access to information indicating that Atta was on a U.S. government "watch list" for terrorist activities. Shortly before his scheduled court date, Atta applied for and received a Florida driver's license. However, he failed to appear in court on May 28, and authorities issued a criminal bench warrant for his arrest... (National Governors Association [NGA], 2002)

By mid-October of that year, it was learned that in July 2001, with the Broward County bench warrant still active, Atta was stopped for another traffic violation in neighboring Palm Beach County. The July traffic stop was by police in Delray Beach, just a few miles over the county line. [1] Because information about low-level arrest warrants was not shared between Florida counties, Delray Beach police did not know that Atta was wanted, nor did they have access to information that would have alerted them to Atta's federal watch list status ("Better Warrant System," 2001).

> On September 11, Atta, despite having an outstanding warrant for his arrest and despite being on a government watch list, boarded a plane in Portland, Maine, using his recently issued Florida driver's license. Authorities believe Atta was at the controls of one of the planes that crashed into the World Trade Centers. (NGA, 2002)

---

[1] Some reports have placed this traffic stop in a different jurisdiction. However, in a meeting with the author on December 2, 2004, Delray Beach Police Chief Joseph L. Schroeder confirmed that it was his officers who stopped Atta in July 2001.

This single event begs questions about how the course of history might have changed if federal-level intelligence information (the terrorist watch list) or low-level, local police information (the bench warrant) had been available to Broward and Palm Beach counties' law enforcement officers. Atta might have been arrested, searched, and questioned; his plans might have been disrupted; his conspirators revealed.

THE FOCUS ON SHARING LOW-LEVEL INFORMATION

The "what if" hindsight analysis of Atta's traffic stop reflects the potential value of low-level law enforcement information to homeland security efforts. In the post-9/11 world, police information has been explicitly incorporated into national counterterrorism policy through the White House's 2007 *National Strategy for Information Sharing* ("*Information Sharing Strategy*"). This strategy recognizes the potential for "traffic tickets and terrorists" connections. These connections can be made by sharing the low-level information that is generated through routine, "all crimes" or "all hazards" police operations and investigations (pg. A1-1).

The *Information Sharing Strategy* offers examples of narcotics, robbery, and cigarette smuggling investigations by local police that produced information leading to the identification of terrorist "cells" (pg.10). In combination with the knowledge that Mohamed Atta slipped through information sharing cracks in 2001, convincing evidence is provided that sharing low-level, local law enforcement information can strengthen America's homeland security.

Of course, this low-level information, alone, does not provide all that is needed to build actionable intelligence in a world of global terror organizations. In the information sharing context, post-9/11 inquiries identified barriers and lapses between federal law enforcement and intelligence agencies that contributed mightily to the terrorists' ability to plan and execute their attacks (e.g., the "9/11 Commission's" 2004 *Final Report of the National Commission on Terrorist Attacks Upon the United States*). Considerable effort has been directed to eliminating these federal-to-federal gaps. This includes the formation of the Department of Homeland Security to consolidate federal agencies (Bush, 2002), the passage of the *Intelligence Reform and Terrorism*

Prevention Act of 2004 (*"Intelligence Reform Act"*), and continuing debate about the *Foreign Intelligence Surveillance Act* (FISA) and its restrictions on the exchange of information between intelligence and law enforcement interests in domestic and foreign operations (Bazan, 2007).

In addition, contemporary counterterrorism intelligence strategy incorporates shared information drawn from non-law enforcement sources, both public and private. Public sources can include information drawn from public utilities or hospitals that might provide forewarning of bioterrorism plots. Private sources can include owners of critical infrastructure such as buildings or computer networks that are vulnerable to both physical and cyber attacks (e.g., GAO, 2003; Markle Foundation, 2003). Collectively, information from public and private sources; local, state, tribal, and federal; law enforcement and non-law enforcement; is envisioned within an "Information Sharing Environment" or "ISE" to support counterterrorism intelligence components (*Intelligence Reform Act*, §1016).

It is critical to note that the value of sharing low-level information in an ISE is *believed* to extend beyond the hunt for terrorists. Information sharing is also expected to benefit public safety, generally, in "traditional" crime control efforts to identify robbers, burglars, sex offenders, etc. The fact is that all terrorists are criminals, but not all criminals are terrorists. With this in mind, post-9/11 information sharing policy has evolved to incorporate the all-crimes or all-hazards perspective. This perspective predicts that law enforcement information sharing can help catch *all* kinds of criminals and, in the mix, some terrorists will be found (e.g., *Information Sharing Strategy*, 2007; Global Justice Information Sharing Initiative [Global], 2004).

The all-crimes approach to information sharing has received increasing attention since 2001. The 2004 publication of *Law Enforcement Intelligence: A Guide for State, Local, and Tribal Law Enforcement Agencies* (Carter, 2004), articulates that low-level data provides the raw information that is critical to developing both counterterrorism intelligence and fighting crime on the local level. The *National Criminal Intelligence Sharing Plan* (NCISP) emphasizes this link, and quotes President Bush asserting that "All across our country we'll be able to tie our terrorist information to local information banks so that the front line of defeating terror becomes activated and real, and those are the local law enforcement officials" (Global, 2004, p. iii).

The NCISP explicitly identifies police information sharing as "...a key tool that law enforcement agencies can employ to support their crime fighting and public safety efforts... this is information that will help [the officers on the streets] do their job" (p iii) and, in an update, notes the value of shared information to intelligence-led policing (Global, 2005). In addition, contemporary policy emphasizes the value of combining both low-level police information and high-level intelligence sources in Fusion Centers that support both all-crimes and counterterrorism intelligence operations (Global, n.d.).

However, the relationship of the information sharing gap to all-crimes policing was a concern long before terrorism shaped a new operational landscape for U.S. police leaders. The ability of criminals to offend undetected across jurisdictions has perplexed police and researchers for many years. Assumptions about criminal mobility have been based largely on data gathered from offenders who have been arrested, with the mobility patterns of those *not* arrested a matter of speculation (Burton et al, 2002). Further, the concept of criminal mobility continues to change. While transportation systems and urban structure have been long-recognized as enabling offenders to commit crimes across police jurisdictions (Brantingham & Brantingham, 1984; Rengert, Piquero & Jones, 1999), the widespread availability of the Internet has created a new category of multi-jurisdictional offenders for whom "time and place" are meaningless (Hinduja, 2004).

These changes in the offending environment coincide with the contemporary police focus (both before and after 9/11) on data-driven or intelligence-led policing. These strategies rely on analysis capabilities, and the analysis capacity of any police agency is dependent on the information available for that purpose (Faggiani & McLaughlin, 1999; Markle Foundation, 2003). Thus, sharing low-level, local policing information is seen as a key to protecting America from *all* kinds of criminals. As noted in the summary of the *National Criminal Intelligence Sharing Plan*, the move to share information is "...a concerted effort by American law enforcement agencies to correct the inadequacies and barriers that impede information and intelligence sharing—so that future tragedies [can] be prevented." (p.1)

The Problem: "We don't know what we don't know."

In transcripts of a 2002 meeting with leaders of military and veterans' service organizations, former Secretary of Defense Donald Rumsfeld notes that, because America has poor law enforcement and intelligence sharing "...we don't know what we don't know..." about information that is available but not shared (U.S. Department of Defense, 2002). In other words, from the perspective of the law enforcement and intelligence communities, the information sharing gap is so wide that the value of closing the gap has been a matter of speculation.

In a time when Google, iPhones, and daycare webcams are commonplace, it is difficult to understand why America's public safety agencies have been unable to share information. However, the reality is that they have not, and there have therefore been very few opportunities for researchers to objectively study the value of information sharing or to suggest how that value (if any was found) might be improved. The pages ahead, however, detail an effort to fill that research void.

This book reports on research that begins to substitute knowledge for "what we don't know" about the value of information sharing. This research encompasses several types of data and observations from the study of FINDER (Florida Integrated Network for Data Exchange and Retrieval) and its users. FINDER is one of the nation's small numbers of operational police information sharing systems.

The value of sharing low-level police information was measured in terms of FINDER's contributions to successful policing outcomes for its 1,600 users. In addition, a variety of user-specific factors was examined to estimate their influence on FINDER-related successes. Thus, both the value of sharing low-level information and ways to increase that value were identified.

The study of a single police information system is not likely to provide compelling evidence that low-level police information sharing will identify terrorists. However, that link has already been suggested by anecdote and codified in policy and law. What the FINDER study *does* show is that sharing low-level information works. It helps solve cases and put criminals in jail.

A final example is offered of the connection between the routine information collected by local police and national security interests. In 2006 the author gave a demonstration of FINDER at an international conference of law enforcement analysts. Prior to the demonstration, a supervisory federal law enforcement agent was engaged in a good-natured debate about the value of FINDER compared to the agent's national, counterterrorism information sharing project. The agent was not convinced that working to share routine police information represented a good investment of counterterrorism resources.

During the demonstration the law enforcement audience was offered an opportunity to query FINDER for any persons of interest. The federal agent provided a name; FINDER returned information on the subject from a 2005 "field contact" reported by police on the Daytona Beach boardwalk. The federal agent – literally drop-jawed – exclaimed "That's him! I've been looking for him for two years!"

Sharing information helps break-down knowledge barriers that previously allowed offenders to move from jurisdiction to jurisdiction without notice. An understanding of the dynamics of information flow, and how investigators and analysts productively use this information, is expected to advance both the all-crimes and counterterrorism efforts of the U.S. law enforcement and intelligence communities.[2]

---

[2] The author has been involved in the development, management, and expansion of FINDER since its inception.

CHAPTER 2

Information Sharing Basics & FINDER

With the link between sharing low-level police information and both all-crimes and counterterrorism public safety interests in mind, it is important to precisely define "low-level police information sharing." This type of information sharing is unique to policing and must be distinguished from other types of information exchanges that occur either exclusively between law enforcement agencies or between law enforcement agencies and other justice system components.

First, the use of the word "information" requires clarification. With apologies to knowledge management purists (e.g., Ackoff, 1989), "information" in this book refers to both data and information. In the applied context of low-level police information, the distinction between data and information is not particularly important. However, it must be noted that "information" is distinct from "intelligence." This book is not about intelligence sharing (see Peterson, 2005, for a succinct discussion of the differences between information and intelligence).

Second, the sets of information that comprise "low-level" police information must be identified. While some examples of low-level information were provided in Chapter 1, this term has only recently appeared in the research literature (Reynolds et al, 2005, 2006) and requires amplification. A good starting point is to look at what is *not* low-level information sharing.

THE NCIC

The tremendous value of sharing even limited sets of police information has been amply demonstrated for almost forty years through the operation of the FBI's National Crime Information Center (NCIC). American police would probably find it impossible to perform their contemporary duties without the ability to conduct the nationwide, electronic searches for the crime-related records that the NCIC provides. It is the NCIC (or a parallel state system) that police typically use to "run a check" on people or property of interest.

By 2002, the NCIC was logging over three million police queries *per day* from U.S. law enforcement agencies (FBI, 2002) and nearly five million per day by 2005 (FBI, 2005b). However, the NCIC is limited to eighteen structured data sets. These data sets include active files of wanted and missing persons, stolen vehicles, identifiable stolen property, criminal history information, and special databases such as sex offenders, gangs, and terror suspects (FBI, 2005a).

The NCIC collects an exclusive set of data designed to address specific information needs such as checking for a warrant, determining whether a car is stolen, or looking at a person's arrest history. The NCIC is purpose-built to meet law enforcement information sharing needs within specific and exclusive parameters. Similarly, the ViCAP (Violent Criminal Apprehension Program) collects and shares 189 specific sets of data about violent crimes. ViCAP was purpose-built in an effort to track violent criminals (Witzig, 2003).

While both the NCIC and ViCAP are critically important law enforcement information sharing systems, they are *not* low-level police information systems. This is because they collect exclusive, regulated sets of information for specific purposes.[1] However, it would also be inaccurate to consider the NCIC and ViCAP as sharing just "high-level" information. In fact, the information found in the NCIC and ViCAP is likely to also be found in low-level information sharing systems. This point will be clarified in later pages.

CJIS-TYPE SYSTEMS

It is also important to understand the distinction between "*police* information sharing" and other forms of "*justice* information sharing." For example, "Justice" or "Integrated Justice" information sharing is

---

[1] The NCIC is not exclusively a police system. It also provides non-police justice data that includes courts and corrections sources.

commonly referenced as "IJIS" (or "ICJIS") and represents integrated justice or integrated criminal justice information sharing.

IJIS projects may be easily confused with police information sharing. For instance, during 2004 and 2005, the author met with a variety of Congressional members and Florida legislators and their staffs to discuss funding for police information sharing. These meetings revealed widespread confusion about the difference between police information sharing and ICJIS projects. Further, the confusion called to question whether homeland security funds were being applied to their proper purposes.

The IJIS model incorporates data exchange between courts, police, corrections, and their various sub-units (e.g., probation and parole; clerks of courts; prosecutors). Thus, a primary goal of the IJIS information sharing model is to facilitate justice *administration*. The "police information sharing" term addresses information exchange *exclusively* among police agencies with crime-solving or intelligence development objectives.

While police may contribute information to IJIS projects, these projects are not "police information sharing" and are not addressed in this book. The reader is referred to the Integrated Justice Information Systems Institute for an overview of the IJIS model and related projects (http://www.ijis.org/rs/home).

LOW-LEVEL POLICE INFORMATION

Having provided examples of what low-level police information *isn't*, the discussion can turn to what it *is*. Reynolds et al (2005) describe low-level information as including:

> ... the vast bulk of information collected by law enforcement and generally stored in automated records management systems. These may include information on suspects, witnesses, pawnshop transactions, vehicle stops, field interviews, suspicious vehicles, towed vehicles, criminal incident reports, non-criminal incident reports, calls for service, property, evidence, and other types of police notes or records (p 129).

Some annotated examples of low-level information, drawn from the FINDER database of several hundred information fields, are provided in Table 2-1. These examples demonstrate the routine quality of low-level information. The information fields represent both criminal and non-criminal incidents, administrative actions, and other information that serves no particular law enforcement purpose other than to document what police are doing during their workday.

When police agencies employ Computer-Aided Dispatch (CAD) and/or automated Records Management Systems (RMS), these low-level bits of information are routinely captured through calls for service, incident reports, traffic citations, and activity logs. However, since police agencies typically do not have interconnected RMS, the information is not shared between jurisdictions (Reynolds et al, 2005, 2006).

To expound on the relationship of information-collected to information-shared, a single police agency's NCIC contributions were compared to that agency's RMS collection. The agency's RMS logged just over one million "events" in a single year. These events represented all reported police activity. Of the million events, roughly 28,800 (2.8%) resulted in NCIC submissions (Scott, 2004). In other words, information about more than 97% of the events in that jurisdiction was *not* shared through the NCIC, law enforcement's premiere information sharing system.

In addition, each event is comprised of numerous pieces of information that may have stand-alone value. For example, a single burglary report includes MO information, suspect information, victim information, witness information, and stolen property information that is not usually eligible for the NCIC. [2] A single traffic stop can include information about time and place, the vehicle, and each occupant. Even a barking-dog complaint produces information about people (the complainant and/or dog owner) and time and place.

---

[2] Information about property that is not uniquely identifiable (e.g., by serial number or other unique marking or description) is usually not submitted to the NCIC.

Table 2-1: Selected Low-level Data Fields from FINDER System (2006)

911NON EMERG	BAKER ACT	FALSE ID GIVEN	PAWN
ABANDONED AUTOS	BOMB DEVICE	FALSE REPORT	PERSN OF INTREST
ACC DMG TO VEH/PROP	BOOKED ADULT	FIELD INFOREPORT	PROWLER
ACCIDENTAL DEATH	CAREER CRIMINAL	FISHING VIOLATION	RECKLESS DRIVER
UNATTNDED VEH	CHECK WELL BEING	FOUND PROPERTY	REPOSSES SION
ADMIN ASSIGNMNT	CHILD PRO-TECT SVC	IMPND AUTO NON-CRIMNL	RUNAWAY
AFFRAY-	CITIZEN ASSIST	LITTERING	SPECIAL NEEDS
AIRCRAFT ACCIDENT	CITIZEN INTELLGNCE	LOST/FOUND VEH TAGS -	STOP PMT ON CHECK
ALARM AUDIBLE	CIVIL DISPUTE	LOST-PERSONS	SUICIDE
ALCOHOL BY PER <21	CONFISCTED PROPERTY -	MEDICAL ONLY	SUSP HAZARD
FIRES-NOT ARSON	ORDINANCE VIOLATED	MEDICAL SECURITY	SUSP INCIDENT
ANIMAL CALLS	COUNTY PROBATION	MENTALLY ILL SUBJ	SUSP PERSON
ALTER LIC PLATE	CULP NEG W/INJURY	MUTUAL AID	SUSP VEHICLE
ALTER INTL REG CARD	DISPLAY ID OF ANOTHER	NATURAL DEATH	TRESPASS WARNING
AREA PATROL	DISTURBNCE	NATURAL DISASTER	UNLAW-FUL ID
ASSIST FD	FAIL TO REG MTR VEH	OFFENSE REPORT	INJUNCTN DOMESTIC
BACKUP NON EMER	FAKE LIC PLATES/	PARKING VIOL	WARRANT

Virtually all of this information is low-level. While some details may be incorporated into NCIC submissions, most reside – unshared – in the collecting agency's RMS.

Definition: Low-level Police Information Sharing

Given the distinction between IJIS-type systems, systems like the NCIC, and low-level information, only "sharing" requires discussion to provide the full definition of low-level police information sharing. For the purpose of the study reported here, "sharing" means the *automated, bi-directional exchange of information*. This study does not consider an agency involved in information sharing unless it is both contributing its own information and accessing other agencies' information. Further, as noted in the IJIS discussion, this study looks only at sharing between police agencies. This includes law enforcement entities at the city, county, state, tribal, and federal levels. Thus, low-level police information sharing is defined as: the automated, bi-directional exchange of low-level information between police agencies.

FINDER

FINDER, the Florida Integrated Network for Data Exchange and Retrieval, is a low-level police information sharing technology and system created by a consortium of Florida law enforcement agencies (the Florida Law Enforcement Data Sharing Consortium) and the University of Central Florida (UCF). FINDER was managed through the Public Safety Technology Center at UCF from its inception in 2002 until 2007 when it was placed in the hands of the Center for Law Enforcement Technology, Training, & Research (LETTR), a non-profit corporation (LETTR, 2008; also see Reynolds et al, 2005, 2006).

FINDER shares only low-level police information between police agencies and encompasses a large and diverse service group of agencies and users. As of mid-2006, when this study was conducted, FINDER involved approximately 60 Florida police agencies that were exchanging low-level information. In addition, at least 60 other agencies had individual users authorized to make queries to FINDER, but those agencies were not yet engaged in contributing to the information exchange.

About 30% of Florida's 400 or so police agencies were involved in FINDER in 2006. Based on July 2004 estimates of populations in counties where member agencies are located, FINDER jurisdictions serviced about 63% of Florida's population (U.S. Census Bureau, 2005). Agencies participating in FINDER were distributed across the state but were concentrated in Central Florida (LETTR, 2008).

In a very broad sense, FINDER operates in a Google-like fashion. FINDER is a web-based, distributed architecture. This means that each participating agency controls which parts of its RMS information are visible to other FINDER members. There is not a data warehouse that stores all of the participants' information. The shared information is not "entered" into the system through keystrokes on a computer. Rather, the information being shared has already been collected by the member agency and stored in its RMS (LETTR, 2008).

There are two important technology functions associated with FINDER that established it as a valuable research environment. First, beginning in December 2004, each individual query to the FINDER system was recorded in a "Query Log" database. The Query Log captured the date and time of the query and identified the agencies to which the query was directed, which user made the query, and the specific parameters of the query (the parameters are what the user was asking about, such as "John Smith" or "red Ford truck"). In other words, the Query Log provided detailed *system use* information.

However, one drawback to FINDER's distributed architecture is that information about individual users is maintained at each agency and is not centrally available. Thus, there is no system-wide ability to establish the number of users with system access or to know anything about these users. Consequently, only an estimate of the number of FINDER users was available through an analysis of the Query Logs. As of February 2006, at least 1,603 users had logged onto the system.

Second, a feature was added to FINDER in 2004 that is referred to as "Success Tagging." When a user makes a query that returns useful information, a point-and-click button appears that is labeled "Click here to tag this report for successes." This button, the "Success Tag" button, takes the user to a pop-up window. The pop-up window asks the user to describe the success that the user is choosing to report.

The requested success information includes a brief text description of the success and automatically references the success tag to the source data that the user has queried.   Thus, subject to the user's inclination, FINDER collects specific, *user-level success* information.

FINDER's attributes suggest that the system is well suited for a study of the value of low-level police information sharing.

- FINDER meets the definition of a police information sharing system: it involves the automated, bi-directional exchange of low-level information between police agencies.
- FINDER's four-year operational history provides an opportunity for longitudinal study.
- FINDER encompasses a relatively large number of agencies that police a sizeable and diverse population.
- The population of FINDER users was estimated at least 1,600. This number of users provides the opportunity for statistically-valid sampling and analysis.
- FINDER captures system use information that provides objective data about how FINDER users employ shared information.
- FINDER's success tag feature captures specific information about user-level successes with shared information.   The Success Tags provide an excellent opportunity to assess information sharing value at the user level.

By 2006 FINDER's Query Logs had captured information about more than 1.8 million system queries, and nearly 800 "successes" had been logged via the Success Tag feature (FINDER, 2006).   The system's users – the members of the Florida Data Sharing Consortium – were enthusiastic about FINDER's contributions to the law enforcement community, and the number of police agencies participating in FINDER grew steadily.

FINDER was ripe for a study of the value of police information sharing.   In February 2006, the Data Sharing Consortium and the University of Central Florida approved a FINDER study that encompassed the collection of data from Query Logs, Success Tags, the Public Safety Technology Center, and the system's users (LETTR, 2008).

CHAPTER 3

The Call for Research: Building the FINDER Study

There have been efforts for at least forty years to share various types of law enforcement information. As noted earlier, perhaps the best example of effective (but limited) sharing is the NCIC. Established in 1967, the NCIC provides a critical information connection to American law enforcement agencies (FBI, 2005a). Other projects, however, have been less successful.

For example, the National Incident Based Reporting System (NIBRS) grew out of a Bureau of Justice Statistics (BJS) award to the FBI in 1982 to develop disaggregated, detailed crime data. NIBRS recognized that important details about crimes were not being shared and that this hindered police understanding of and response to multi-jurisdictional crime trends (Dunworth, 2000; Faggiani & McLaughlin, 1999).

BJS developed a data collection format that was published to law enforcement agencies across the nation. Police agencies were asked to voluntarily submit the specified NIBRS data. By 1996, however, the jurisdictions participating in NIBRS represented less than 6% of the nation's population, and the BJS authorized a study to determine the cause of low participation rates. The study revealed that state and local agencies chose not to support NIBRS because of its unfunded drain on local resources and the perceived absence of NIBRS benefits at the local level (BJS, 1997, 2005; Dunworth, 2000; Faggiani & McLaughlin, 1999; FBI, 2007).

The Violent Criminal Apprehension Program (ViCAP) mentioned earlier offers another example of a pre-9/11, national effort to share important information that is not captured by the NCIC or other systems. ViCAP was created by the FBI in 1985 as a database of details about violent criminal acts. The database requires local police agencies to complete the 189-item form about violent crimes and suspects. By 1996, however, less than 7% of the eligible violent crime information was being submitted. Lackluster participation in ViCAP has been attributed to the promise of its benefits being outweighed by its expense to local agencies (Witzig, 2003).

Local and regional projects have also had problems. In 1999, a number of St. Louis-area agencies formed the now-defunct Gateway information sharing project (DOJ, 2002). The failure of Gateway has been attributedto the loss of project champions and local commitment.[1] In mid-2001, a statewide Florida project that shared pawn-shop information among police was shut down through political pressure applied by gun rights activists (Moore, 2001).

Post-9/11 police information sharing efforts have also suffered setbacks. Issues surrounding politics, organization, technology, and funding have been identified as obstacles. Examples of this include the MATRIX project (Multistate Anti Terrorism Information Exchange), which envisioned interstate information sharing between police intelligence components. MATRIX provided for sharing a mix of publicly-available and law enforcement-restricted information. However, this project attracted the interest of organizations concerned about privacy issues, and the ensuing media attention and political fallout resulted in the project's discontinuation after less than two years in operation (Florida Department of Law Enforcement [FDLE], 2005).

A failed FBI project that was initiated post-9/11 also attracted considerable media and political attention. The FBI's $170-million effort to build its intra- and inter-agency information exchange capacity illustrates how technology planning problems can thwart information sharing. The failure was attributed primarily to poor technology planning processes that included a lack of focus on the end users' needs (McGroddy & Lin, 2004).

A lack of understanding end users' needs and objectives also contributed to the dissolution of a project that provided for information sharing between local and federal intelligence officials. In 2005, a

---

[1] This information was obtained via discussions with former Gateway participants.

disagreement on the types of information to be shared – and by whom – caused problems.

A law enforcement oversight board comprised of local officials pulled the Joint Regional Information Exchange System (JRIES) from a planned integration with the Department of Homeland Security's (DHS) Homeland Security Information Network (HSIN). The inclusion of JRIES in the HSIN had been expected to provide the core of HSIN information sharing capacity, but JRIES officials were concerned that the HSIN would provide sensitive information to non-law enforcement users. The departure of JRIES left the fate of the HSIN in doubt (Lipowicz, 2005; U.S. House Committee on Homeland Security Democratic Staff, 2006).

Unfortunately, there is little research available to describe these problematic information sharing projects and their related lessons-learned. Their disappearance or disappointing returns reflect an environment that has offered few opportunities for information sharing research.

It is in this research-poor environment that post 9/11 police leaders have been faced with making decisions about the relationship between the cost and value of information sharing. Only in recent years has there been a call for research-based evidence to determine the benefits of police information sharing– if any – and to help establish whether it serves its intended crime-fighting purposes (BJA, 2005).

The research deficit was described in 2005 by the Comprehensive Regional Information Sharing Project (CRISP), an effort funded through the Department of Justice:

> Currently, many state and local law enforcement agencies obligate large portions of their yearly operational budgets in support and development of multi-jurisdictional information sharing systems (ISSs). However to date, no single document or system analysis has been developed that maps or describes how multi-jurisdictional ISSs work. During 2005 and extending into 2006, the CRISP project is beginning to address this need by evaluating and documenting the information exchanges of selected operational ISSs around the country, to determine their benefit to street-level law enforcement. The project is addressing both technical and functional characteristics of each ISS, how the ISS supports

policing functions, and what specific information is being delivered to law enforcement officers on the street (Mitretek, 2005).[2]

CRISP affirmed the importance of understanding performance in police information sharing *and* the absence of research providing evidence of effective policy or systems.

Similarly, the BJA called for "outcome evaluations" that assess the performance of police information sharing. The BJA noted that past research focused on user evaluations, user perceptions, or system case studies versus measurable outcomes. The BJA attributed the lack of outcome or success-based research to the "newness" of the police information sharing push (BJA, 2005). It was in this new field of study that the FINDER system presented a promising research opportunity.

THE ARJIS STUDY

The BJA Center for Program Evaluation (BJA, 2005) provides a reference list of roughly seventy publications identified as relevant to police information sharing research. While these publications are not individually discussed here, a review of them suggests that none are oriented to objectively measure or predict actual outcomes attributed to the exchange of low-level police information. Rather, these publications tend to focus on the organizational dynamics of *justice* information sharing systems (e.g., BJA, 2002), the technologies or potential technologies underpinning information sharing (e.g., Hauck et al, 2001), or the prospective preferences of police for information sharing system design (e.g., Chen et al, 2002).

A search was conducted of the scholarly, professional, and popular literature in an effort to identify police information projects and any related outcome evaluations or research. The search, conducted in 2005, included over 4,000 articles, publications, or websites that appeared relevant to police information sharing (Scott, 2005). This search produced information about only one project, ARJIS, that appears to have been the topic of an outcome-focused research effort.

---

[2] Mitretek became Noblis in 2007 (see www.noblis.org).

By 2007 the ARJIS study still appeared as the foundation for national approaches to information sharing research (Noblis, 2006).

The ARJIS study was structured by Zaworski (2004) as a comparison between a non-sharing police agency in Florida and agencies participating in a form of information sharing via the San Diego ARJIS (Area Regional Justice Information Sharing) project. Although ARJIS is a *justice* (versus *police*) project, Zaworski focused on police data.

Zaworski (2004) relied primarily on user perceptions, expectations, and user-recall about the value of information sharing (and technology in general) to individual performance. He did not include objective measures of individual performance. He did make an effort to link information sharing to *agency level,* objective performance measures; in this case, aggregate crime solving and arrest rates found in the Uniform Crime Reports (UCR). Zaworski found no significant difference between the sharing/non-sharing agencies in the aggregate performance measures and concluded that a police agency's management priorities, versus information sharing, may have the greater effect on aggregate crime control measures.

While Zaworski's (2004) findings seem to show that police information sharing lacks demonstrated (as opposed to perceived) crime-solving value, it is important to note that he was contrasting individual user's perceptions against agencies' aggregate crime statistics. Zaworski recognized the link from the individual to the aggregate as tenuous and elaborated on the difficulty of collecting good user performance data in the applied setting. Unfortunately, Zaworski's reliance on UCR data was later diminished with the discovery of UCR manipulation by officers in one of the studied agencies (Smith, 2004).

However, Zaworski's (2004) research remains important. First, he collected a large sample (600 users) of baseline data on user perceptions related to the individual value of police information sharing. This provided a foundation for collecting additional user perception data through FINDER and linking it to strong performance measures. The link could provide a better understanding of relationships between user perceptions and actual performance.

Second, Zaworski examined potential relationships between user characteristics and perceptions of individual performance. These characteristics (such as education, training, and experience) provided a starting point in building a FINDER-based research framework.

Third, the ARJIS study considers information sharing *system use*. Zaworski's data indicates a strong link between users' reports of system use and their perceptions of information sharing value. The presence of objective system use data in FINDER (the Query Logs) suggested an opportunity to further explore the system use/individual performance connection.

Zaworski's (2004) findings are similar to that of technology systems research in both police and non-police environments. Lin (2004), for instance, studied police use of emerging technology and their perceptions of its value. Lin found (not surprisingly) that police detectives reported their intent to use a technology system that fulfilled their task needs: investigating and solving crime. Further, Lin reported that these detectives would use the system even if it were difficult to use or required significant training. Although Lin did not attempt to identify individual performance measures related to the technology, Lin's findings parallel those of Zaworski: police report that they will use technology systems that help them perform their jobs.

Other research affirms the link between user-perceived benefit and the police user's intended use of technology systems. Ioimo (2000) and Ioimo and Aronson (2003) found significant relationships between user expectations of success and the use of mobile computing systems. Colvin and Goh (2005) explored factors of police officers' acceptance and intended use of new technology related to its officer safety value, and Nunn and Quinet (2002) tried to examine the relationship between actual system use and the system's contribution to meeting community policing goals.

In each of these research efforts that address the *prospective* use of information systems, specific outcomes or objective performance measures of technology use were not captured, but the researchers concluded that police would not use a technology system that failed to address their pragmatic policing needs. Conversely, these researchers generally concur that police report the *intent* to use technology that *does* meet their policing needs. This link between police users' needs and system use was important to the FINDER study approach.

The FINDER Research Framework

The call for police information sharing research emphasizes the need for objective measures of its value. Thus, the initial question in the FINDER study was "What value does FINDER provide?" However, "value" is a contextual term, so a critical step to using the FINDER system as the subject of study was to operationalize the concept of value in the FINDER context. Learning from Zaworski's (2004) difficulties using aggregate estimates of value (agency UCR statistics), an initial *user-level* measure of value was conceived. This measure is *user-level success*.

User-level success is an important issue for police leaders and policy makers. In practical terms, police chiefs and sheriffs want information sharing that detectives and officers can use to fight crime. Each individual "success" represents a case of the detectives and officers doing just that. Thus, the unit of analysis in this study is the individual FINDER user. In the larger picture, the aggregate of these successes should translate to agency, community, regional, and national information sharing value.

However, the research literature indicated that measuring "success" with technology systems is a complex and difficult task because success is relative to both the user and the system (Goodhue, 1995, 1998; Goodhue & Thompson, 1995). This task may be particularly difficult in the context of police technology systems (Nunn, 2001; Nunn & Quinet, 2002; Zaworski, 2004), and there are no commonly accepted measures of user-level success identified by researchers. Instead, the users' *intended* or *perceived* frequency of system use (Davis, 1989; Nunn & Quinet, 2002; Venkatesh & Davis, 2000) or the users' *perceptions* of how the system affects their performance (Goodhue, 1995; 1998; Goodhue & Thompson, 1995; Zaworski, 2004) are frequently considered as surrogate, or substitute, measures of success.

These surrogate measures of success are not believed to be entirely adequate for gauging the benefits of police information sharing (BJA, 2005). Thus, this study was designed to move beyond the surrogates and identify objective, user-level success measures. The FINDER measures of user-level success in this study are characterized as "metrics." Metrics are standards that help assess performance levels and require specific, measurable, attainable, realistic, and timely data

(U.S. Department of Energy, 1995; also see Noblis, 2006). Data available about FINDER's users appeared to provide a good environment for metric development.

First, as noted earlier, FINDER users can capture their success experiences using the Success Tag reporting function of the FINDER software. The Success Tag reports were available as part of this study. Preliminary exploration of the Success Tag records revealed great variation in the level of reported successes among FINDER users. This variation was important because it suggested differences among the users and lent itself to building a success metric. The existence of differences between more successful and less successful FINDER users was fundamental to the study. Theoretically, "good" differences between users might be exploited and "bad" differences suppressed in order to improve the value of police information sharing.

Second, also noted earlier, the FINDER system automatically records information about system use in detailed "Query Logs" that provide a record about each user's FINDER activity. Levels of system use are one of the surrogate measures for system success discussed above (e.g., Davis, 1989; Goodhue, 1995). Integrating system use data from the Query Logs with users' Success Tag reports permitted an expansion of prior concepts of user-level performance measurement.

The user-level success metric must have some applied value if it is to be relevant to police and policy makers. As noted above, the ability to identify differences between more successful and less successful police information users suggests an opportunity: understanding those differences may permit crafting a more productive information sharing environment. To guide an exploration of this opportunity, this study employed a research framework based on an adaptation of Goodhue's (1995) Task-Technology Fit model (TTF).

Task-Technology Fit

TTF was selected as the theoretical framework for the FINDER study because of its pragmatic approach to user-level performance. Other models were considered, such as Davis' 1989 Technology Acceptance Model (TAM), Venkatesh & Davis' TAM II (2000), and a variety of approaches that modified or combined TTF, TAM, and related frameworks (e.g., see Legris, Ingham, & Collerette, 2003). However, most of these approaches tend to focus on system "usefulness" or "usability" versus the direct, outcome-focused concept of user-level performance provided by TTF, with TTF appearing more relevant to specific, user-based outcomes in the policing environment. In addition, Zaworski (2004) had used TTF to frame the ARJIS study, and the common framework would lend itself to leveraging Zaworski's work.

The simple form of TTF is depicted in the Figure 3-1 adaptation. This model suggests that technology, user characteristics, and the fit of technology to the user's task needs predict technology use and user-level performance related to that technology.

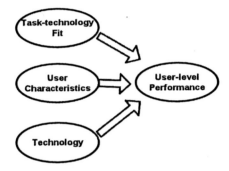

Figure 3-1: Basic Task-Technology Fit Model
(adapted from Goodhue, 1995)

However, Goodhue (1995) acknowledged that a technology task fit and individual performance link is a complicated feedback relationship with complex interactions. He offered an expanded model that included an exploratory link between task fit, *system use*, and user-level performance.

This model, shown in Figure 3-2, suggests that when an information technology satisfies the job tasks of the system's users, they are more likely to use the system (system use) and employ the technology to a positive impact on individual performance. Further, the model assumes the influence of generalized "other factors" (p.1841) that affect system use and that the user has discretion whether and how much the system will be used.

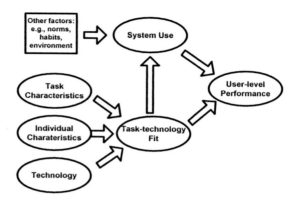

Figure 3-2: TTF Model Exploring System Use
(adapted from Goodhue, 1995)

It is the TTF model in Figure 3-2 that was used to develop the framework for studying FINDER. This model suggested three independent variables (or groupings of variables) that might influence FINDER's user-level successes: the technology (FINDER and other police systems), user characteristics (individual characteristics of FINDER's police users), and technology fit (how well FINDER fits its police users' task needs). Within this framework, and with user-level success as the conceptual measure of information sharing value, the research question was refined to: "What factors influence user-level success in the FINDER system?"

The research used by Goodhue (1995) to support the TTF model involved corporate technologies and working environments, not public safety technologies or policing environments. Thus, the research literature and subject matter experts were consulted to help adapt the TTF factors specifically to the study of police information sharing.

Table 3-1: Task Technology Fit Hypothetical Relationships & Application to FINDER Study

	RELATIONSHIPS IN GOODHUE'S (1995) TTF MODEL	RELATIONSHIPS IN FINDER CONTEXT*
Task Fit	Task Characteristics → Task Technology Fit	User's Job Assignment → User's FINDER task-fit
	Individual Characteristics → Task Tech Fit	User's computer expertise → User's FINDER task-fit
	Technology → Task Technology Fit	None identified – explored as control
System Use	Task Technology Fit → System Use	User's FINDER task-fit → User's Usage Rate (H6) User Job Assignment → User's Usage Rate (H9) Technology Acceptance measure → Usage Rate (H8)
	Other Factors → System Use	FINDER Training → User's Usage Rate (H7)
Performance	Task Technology Fit → Performance	User's FINDER task-fit → User Level Success (H1) User's Job Assignment → User Level Success (H5) User's computer expertise → User Level Success (H3)
	System Use → Performance	User's Usage Rate → User Level Success (H2) FINDER Training → User Level Success (H4)

* Value in parentheses (H*i*) indicates a hypothesis, number *i*, will be proposed.

As a result, a number of observable police and FINDER-based indicator variables were identified that parallel those in the TTF model. For instance, prior research and theory suggested that the FINDER user's job experience, job assignment, and workload would be valid, observable, and measurable indicators of the task-technology fit factor proposed by Goodhue (1995). The user-level success measure could be used to represent "user-level performance" in the TTF model, and so forth.

Table 3-1 aligns TTF-modeled relationships with their parallel relationships in the FINDER context. The alignment of theoretical relationships provided by the TTF model with real-life measures or indicators in FINDER provided the foundation for an initial set of hypotheses. However, while relationships of some sort could be hypothesized with the application of the TTF framework, the nature or direction of the relationships (i.e., positive or negative) could not be proposed until measurable variables were defined. These variables are discussed in the next chapter.

CHAPTER 4

Defining the FINDER Variables

The concepts incorporated in the Task-Technology Fit model (Goodhue, 1995) required translation to the applied realities of the FINDER police information sharing environment. This translation was accomplished with reliance on a mixture of theory, adaptation from prior research, expert advice, logic, and common sense. This process produced an initial set of six dependent and independent study variables, shown in Table 4-1 on page 44, and six control variables, shown in Table 4-2 on page 45. Each variable, and the arguments supporting its definition and measurement, is discussed below.

USER-LEVEL SUCCESS

Goodhue's (1995) "individual performance" term was operationalized as "user-level success." The change in terminology was supported by the FINDER study's basic premise that the user level is the place to look for indicators of police information sharing success. As discussed earlier, FINDER's users can use Success Tags to report outcomes desirable in the user's specific context. User-level definitions of this type may be considered more valuable than terms imposed by administrators, external researchers, or policy makers (Long & Franklin, 2004). Thus, as used in this study, "success" refers to specific outcomes that the *users* consider beneficial and is not intended to assert system-wide success.

Initially, user-level success was operationalized as each instance of a FINDER user reporting a success through the Success Tagging feature. It was thought that a simple count of Success Tags might provide an objective measure for user-level success. However, after preliminary analyses, some difficulties with this approach were anticipated.

First, all of the Success Tag reports in FINDER are due to voluntary self-reporting, and self-reports are subject to a variety of biases. The risk of *social desirability* or *prestige* bias (Alreck & Settle, 1995, p. 100) was of particular concern because a FINDER success could be seen as enhancing the user's self-image or image in the eyes of others.

Second, FINDER-user focus groups that met in October 2004 and November 2005 suggested that FINDER successes might be dramatically *under*-reported.[1] The first group (eleven line-level detectives or squad-level supervisors) convened before the Success Tag feature was available. This group reported consistent levels of "successful" FINDER use. Members of the group said FINDER routinely helped them work more efficiently, clear cases, and acquire information that was not otherwise available. Subsequent informal reports from members of that user group suggested continuing successes over the following year.

However, by the November 2005 focus group meeting, the success tag feature had been in place for almost one year, but reported successes were not reflecting the constant success level asserted by the 2004 focus group. Thus, this topic received considerable attention.

Those FINDER users affirmed that they continued to experience consistent success with the system, but they admitted to only sporadically submitting Success Tag reports. The users in this group, six line-level detectives, gave a number of explanations for the gap between actual and reported successes. These included:

- "I'm not sure what kinds of things you want us to report."
- "I didn't know what the Success Tag button was supposed to be for."
- "No one told me that [success tagging] is important."

---

[1] The first group consisted entirely of members from one Sheriff's Office. The second group included members from several police agencies.

- "I'm too busy to use [success tagging]. You guys should know that, the fact is, I use FINDER all the time, and that's proof that it's successful for me."
- "A lot of times I get a hit [data match] and I keep on going to make my case. Then, by time I finish my case, I forget to do the [success] tag."
- "Everyone on my squad uses it [FINDER] all the time. It works great, but I guarantee you none of them took the time to make a success report."
- "I wouldn't do it [success tagging] because I'm busy. But [names another detective] is always giving me [expletive] about it, so sometimes I go back and try and do the [success] tags when I'm not too busy."

Third, between December 2005 and February 2006, roughly 731 Success Tags were logged relative to 1.8 million queries, or about one success per 2,500 queries. The successes were claimed by approximately 115 (7%) of the system's estimated 1,600 users during that period (FINDER, 2006). It is possible that these 115 success-reporting users were the only users having success; however, that seemed unlikely in light of the focus groups' reports. In addition, the author and FINDER staff were receiving frequent anecdotal accounts of successes that did not appear in the Success Tag reports.

Thus, success tagging records were suspected to be incomplete and, alone, were not logically or statistically sufficient to support empirical testing. Consequently, methods to capture surrogate success measures were considered. These included:

1. Through a user survey, capture success (or performance) *expectations* as a proxy for actual successes.
2. Through a user survey, attempt to determine the relationship of actual successes reported to actual successes experienced, and weight reported successes accordingly.
3. Create a composite success measure using a combination of reported successes, user expectations, and actual system use data.
4. Develop a success construct with confirmatory factor analysis (CFA) using reported successes, user

expectations (or estimates) of success, and actual usage data as the component indicators of the CFA.

The first option is suggested by Goodhue (1995) in TTF measurements that capture the user's expectation of success. Goodhue explicitly recognizes the weaknesses inherent in substituting the user's performance expectations as a "surrogate" for actual performance (p. 105) but notes that there is often no other option in applied research.

The second option encompasses both an objective measure of success and the user's recall of unreported successes. If users (via survey) generally recall, say, five unreported successes for every one success they reported, the number of Success Tags reported could be multiplied by five to estimate the actual success level. While this option incorporates some degree of objectivity, the use of user-recall data may produce questionable results (e.g., Zaworski, 2004).

The third option incorporates known levels of reported successes, known levels of usage, and/or other factors into a summative index. Summative indices are mathematically convenient, while scales require substantial theoretical, logical or expert grounding (Babbie, 1995). Some researchers suggest that a combination of scaled or indexed measures may be the best way to get at a valid (but not entirely objective) technology performance metric.

For example, intended use and/or actual usage data has considerable support as valid proxy measure for user-level performance (e.g., Legris et al, 2003) and could be conceptually defended as a component of a success scale. However, scales built on cumulative values of different components do not necessarily capture the relative importance of its components (Babbie, 1995), and no validated scale was identified that could be directly applied to the FINDER study.

The fourth option incorporates confirmatory factor analysis (CFA). CFA appears appropriate in this study's context since it is intended to "confirm" a theory-driven analysis (Kline, 2005; Maruyama, 1998; Thompson, 2005; Wan, 2002). User-level success can be conceptualized as a theoretically supported construct that is measured through indicators, including actual success, usage, user intentions, and user expectations.

The CFA approach has the advantage of assigning standardized coefficient estimates to the indicators. The standardized estimates report the relative magnitude of the indicators' influence on the success construct. For example, Goodhue (1998) employed CFA in his examination of TTF factors across a wide domain of business technologies, but he did not address a performance metric in that analysis.

However, some researchers believe that factor analyses are frequently misapplied and misinterpreted (Hurley et al, 1997). The TTF theory and FINDER task-fit measure required further investigation and analysis to support a CFA (Goodhue & Thompson, 1995; Goodhue, 1998).

Thus, none of the four options for measuring user-level success were ideal. Each option did, however, provide different perspectives by which a "best" measurement could be obtained. These different perspectives were used to create alternative success-measure items in a user survey instrument (detailed in later chapters) with the intent that a credible measure could be constructed should the Success Tags, alone, not be adequate for empirical analysis.

FINDER TASK-FIT

Goodhue (1995, 1998) and Goodhue and Thompson (1995) developed an instrument intended to measure twelve dimensions that capture how a specific technology fits the user's task needs and environment. The measure of task-fit in this study, which was borrowed from Goodhue's model and was influenced by Zaworski's (2004) expansion of that model, was labeled "FINDER task-fit." This label was intended to clarify that it is a measurement representing a distinct adaptation of Goodhue's instrument, specifically modified for the FINDER-based study. Goodhue anticipated that adaptations of TTF would be necessary in different information system domains, and Zaworski used a TTF adaptation in his comparative study of police information sharing.

Goodhue's (1995) twelve TTF dimensions include (broadly): ease of use, value to user, compatibility to user needs, flexibility, and system reliability. While Goodhue (1998) found the TTF measure a valid predictor of users' *expected* system use and performance gains, he did not link expectations to *actual* performance. Further, Goodhue noted that his validity-testing was limited to a corporate environment and was not necessarily generalizable.

The FINDER task-fit measure was conceptualized as a numerical value derived from a summative index of component, task-fit indicators. The index's components and conceptual relationships of FINDER task-fit dimensions to Goodhue's (1995) TTF dimensions are discussed in detail in Chapter 5.

USAGE RATE

Goodhue's (1995) TTF model seeks to explain performance in terms of task fit *and* system use (see Figure 3-2). In the TTF model, system use is presented as *intended* use and as being positively related to *expected* performance. As previously noted, intended or expected system use is frequently used as a surrogate measure for performance or success (Davis, 1989; Goodhue & Thompson, 1995; Nunn & Quinet, 2002). Logically, if users have a choice, why would they use a technology system that *did not* generate some form of success?

However, assuming a positive relationship between usage and success could be misleading. For example, a user who is required to use a specific system may, effectively, have no technology options, or a user may have access to only one system. Alternatively, the user may have the choice between many similar or complementary technologies. If there are no alternative technology choices available to the user, or use of a particular system is required, usage levels of that system may be high, even if success with that system is low.

If multiple systems are available, use in any one system might be low depending on that user's task needs relative to the task needs of and systems available to other users. In addition, high levels of usage may indicate the user is untrained and inefficient, or that the system is inefficient. Conversely, low levels of usage may indicate very effective users and a very efficient system (e.g., Goodhue, 1995, 1998; Goodhue & Thompson, 1995).

On the other hand, police users consistently report they would use a system if it enabled success, regardless of system difficulty or complexity (e.g., Colvin & Goh, 2005; Lin, 2004). Essentially, and importantly, a complex mix of contextual factors appears to be important to the interpretation of system use. These factors include the user environment, technology, and pragmatic results of system use. This mix of factors affecting system use is modeled, but not explained, in the TTF framework (Goodhue, 1995, 1998; Goodhue & Thompson, 1995).

Another aspect of assessing system use relative to performance may be related to the cross-sectional approach used in prior research

(Goodhue & Thompson, 1995; Nunn & Quinet, 2002). FINDER focus groups asserted that their *continued* use of the system reflects their success experience and expectations. This suggested a time-variant approach to usage that is logical and supported by research (Venkatesh & Davis, 2000; Venkatesh et al, 2003).

A simple measure of usage is the number of FINDER queries made by the user during a given time period. However, query volume alone lacks face validity as a measure. For example, two users might have each made one hundred queries during a six-month period after joining FINDER. Thus, a resultant cross-sectional analysis would find these two users were not different. However, if one user initiated all one hundred queries in the first week and not thereafter, it might be concluded that this user experimented with the system and, finding it unhelpful, never used it again. Alternatively, if the second user queried FINDER at a steadily increasing rate over the six-month period, it would seem this user's needs were being met – evidenced by continuing and increasing use – and a stronger claim of the usage/ user-level success relationship might be supported.

All other influences held constant, the TTF framework suggested the best system use measure as *usage rate over time* versus a cross-sectional "snapshot." Further, as the examples above indicate, the *change in usage rate over time* could be important (i.e., is usage increasing, stable, or decreasing?). Therefore, in order to capture usage as a meaningful measure, *usage rate* was conceptualized as a mathematical function of individual user query volume, time period, and change over time. With the potential of confounding effects in mind and with the support of the literature and FINDER users' input, the usage rate was proposed as being positively related to user-level success.

COMPUTER EXPERTISE

The TTF model (Goodhue, 1995) suggests "individual characteristics" are important in considering task fit. Goodhue described individual characteristics, conceptually, as the user's familiarity with basic computer functions, or "computer literacy" (p 1836). Computer literacy is, presumably, indirectly captured in TTF instrument questions that relate to perceived ease of use or usability, but Goodhue used just a single survey item (familiarity with word processing and spreadsheets) as a computer literacy indicator.

In addition, the author's experience and focus group observations suggested that the computer expertise influence on usage and success might be important. Some users just seem to embrace and successfully use technology much more quickly than others. Thus, this study used a *computer expertise* measure.

The measure is informed by the TTF instrument, Davis' (1989) Technology Acceptance Model (TAM), Venkatesh and Davis' (2000) TAM II, and a review of the computer literacy literature. Zaworski's (2004) computer expertise terminology was borrowed for its existing use in the police information sharing context. This term is used in place of "computer literacy," which encompasses a large body of study (e.g., Kim & Keith, 1994; Smith, Caputi, & Rawstorne, 2000). The computer expertise measure was conceptualized as a numerical value derived from a summative index of items collected by the user survey.

JOB ASSIGNMENT

The TTF model incorporates "task characteristics" into the task technology fit construct. Goodhue and Thompson (1995) assessed the effect of task characteristics on the task technology fit by classifying users into broad job-assignment categories (e.g., administrative, managerial, executive). Clearly, "tasks" are an important component of a model that considers the relationship between technology and its fit to the user's tasks. This relationship has been empirically validated, but tests of TTF have been across dissimilar business environments, and the instrument was developed with diverse business applications in mind. Goodhue notes the lack of job-specificity in the TTF instrument as a limiting factor in its application elsewhere (Goodhue, 1998).

The FINDER context provided an opportunity to focus the task characteristics construct. FINDER's relatively homogenous police context permitted greater specificity in defining task characteristics. Rather than incorporating generalized task sets in the analysis, task characteristics were operationalized by identifying the user's job assignment.

Assessing and understanding the influence of the FINDER user's job assignment on that user's success level was extremely important. For example, does FINDER help resolve large volumes of barking dog complaints (by identifying dog owners) but not provide much value in homicide investigations? Does FINDER help solve child rape offenses and identify emerging terrorist organizations while lending little value to investigating people who make off with grocery shopping carts?

If the policy goal is to fight terrorism, then FINDER (and similar systems) must be designed to support the needs of intelligence officers. If the goal is to enhance sex crimes investigations, then FINDER (and similar systems) must also be designed to meet sex crimes detectives' needs. Because information sharing has not generally been available to either intelligence officers or sex crimes detectives (or to any other officers) in the past, the kinds of information they need, the form of the information, and how (and if) they can use the information successfully has not been established (BJA, 2005).

Two challenges were anticipated in the inclusion of a job assignment variable in this study. First, capturing "job assignment" in an empirical analysis was expected to be problematic. There were hundred of possible job titles among FINDER's users that the user survey would capture as nominal data. However, the literature provided guidance in cataloging police job titles into sets that lend themselves to analysis (Fyfe et al, 1997; Commission on Accreditation of Law Enforcement Agencies [CALEA], 1998). It was anticipated that FINDER users' job titles could be collapsed into meaningful sets suited to empirical analysis.

Second, the TTF model does not specify a direct effect of task characteristics on success or system use. As the TTF model reflects (Figure 3-2), task characteristics have a hypothesized, direct effect on task-fit; task-fit then has a direct effect on both system use and individual performance. Thus, strictly construed, the TTF framework does not predict the effect of job assignment on the performance measures.

However, neither does TTF assume that actual successes, actual usage, or specific job assignments are being measured. In addition, other researchers have demonstrated a direct effect of users' tasks on intended use or expected performance gains (Colvin & Goh, 2005; Lin, 2004; Zaworski, 2004).

Thus, the FINDER user's job assignment was conceptualized as an independent variable with direct effects predicted on the FINDER task-fit measure, system usage, and user-level success.

FINDER TRAINING

The influence of user training on TTF, system use, or performance is not specifically addressed in the TTF model. The literature (Goodhue, 1995, 1998; Goodhue & Thompson, 1995; Davis, 1989; Legris et al, 2003) suggests that user training may be encompassed by technology acceptance and usability measures, but Zaworski (2004) found that several user-training indicators were independently significant to technology fit. Technology fit was expected to help predict both success and system usage.

The training variable in this study was conceptualized as having a *direct* effect on both usage rates and user-level success. An indirect effect, as noted above, is supported by the Goodhue (1995) model. The direct effect was indicated by FINDER-specific anecdotal evidence in combination with a preliminary analysis of use and success data.

The anecdotal evidence arose from a training program that was developed for FINDER users. The trainers, who informally monitored usage and success data, perceived that both usage and reported successes rose almost immediately after users attended the training. A preliminary review of the query log and Success Tag data suggested this perception was accurate, and data was available that outlined if and when specific groups of users received training.

However, the FINDER training curriculum emphasized success tagging and innovative use of the FINDER system. Thus, it was not known whether training actually influenced usage and success versus simply influencing the users' probability of *reporting* successes. In addition, it was not known whether any gains in success experience due to training were sustained over time.

Regardless, the literature supported FINDER-user training as an independent variable that might indirectly influence both system use and success. The best objective evidence (query logs and success reports) suggested a direct effect as well. Thus, FINDER training was included in the research model. Training was operationalized as a dichotomous variable reflecting whether the user had received the training.

CONTROL VARIABLES

There are several variables that are not of primary interest for predictive value in the study framework, but they must be considered to help control for confounding effects or assist in identifying spurious relationships (Senese, 1997). The control variables in this study were identified as the user's law enforcement experience (Zaworski, 2004), the user's time as a FINDER user, the user's agency name and agency size (Davis, 1989; Goodhue, 1995, 1998; Legris et al, 2003; Zaworski, 2004), the user's workload, and the user's access to other technology (Goodhue, 1995, 1998; Goodhue & Thompson, 1995).

Experience

Zaworski's (2004) study found that users' law enforcement tenure was significantly related to their task-fit measures in an information-sharing environment. However, TTF does not specifically link a user's experience (tenure on the job) to the interaction of technology and task. In other words, the influence of the user's job experience on task-fit, use, or performance is not specifically hypothesized by TTF.

Logically, in the FINDER and police contexts, an experienced police officer *should* have higher levels of success than the inexperienced officer, with or without FINDER. However, studies of the relationship between law enforcement experience and technology have shown mixed results (e.g., Danziger & Kraemer, 1985; Zaworski, 2004).

Thus, law enforcement tenure (years of law enforcement related experience) was incorporated as a control variable in this study's design. The inclusion of this variable was believed to be necessary to control for differences in user-level success that could be attributed to user-level proficiencies that were *not* related to FINDER.

Time As User

The inclusion of a time-as-user control was based on the same logic as the law enforcement tenure control variable. Logically, users with more experience using FINDER should have higher levels of success. However, Goodhue and Thompson (1995) and Venkatesh and Davis (2000) found negative relationships with system use from users who, they speculated, were more experienced with the technology or, due to reliance on the technology, more sensitive to any system shortcomings. These findings suggest it is possible that the more seasoned or sophisticated technology users are more difficult to satisfy.

The user's time as a FINDER user was considered important to control for variances (in either direction) in task fit, usage, or success. The time as FINDER user variable was operationalized as a scale measure. The measure was proposed as the number of weeks since the user first logged-in to the FINDER system. These data were available through the FINDER query logs.

Agency Name

The user's agency (identified by agency name) was included to represent the user's general task environment. This variable was envisioned as indirectly capturing the subjective norms and other contextual influences suggested by the TTF model. As a practical matter, it was recognized as unlikely that the agency name could be used in a parametric analysis. This is a nominal variable, and there were at least 120 agencies involved in FINDER. However, agency name was expected to have value in non-parametric analyses.

A preliminary review of usage and success data suggested that certain agencies produced high levels of both use and success reports. The author's observations suggested that these high levels of usage and success reporting were due to the presence of a FINDER advocate in those agencies. Thus, exploratory value was associated with capturing the user's agency name and, potentially, controlling for unique contextual influences associated with the agency.

Agency Size

The user's agency size (number of sworn officers) can be linked to the availability of technology resources and support in police agencies (Nunn, 2001). IT resources and support are believed to influence task-fit perceptions (Goodhue, 1995), and any influence on task-fit was important to recognize in the design of this study.

The inclusion of an agency-size variable as an indicator of IT resources and support was expected to help control for related variances in task-fit measures. In addition, information about the user's agency size was used to help assess the representativeness of user survey responses. This assessment was to be based on survey response rates that were proportional to the agency size distribution of those agencies involved with FINDER.

Number of Agencies Sharing Information

In the TTF model, Goodhue (1995, 1998) discusses the effect of information bring available from multiple systems on individual performance. In the corporate context studied by Goodhue, the multiple systems were intra-organizational (such as systems in different divisions of the same corporation) versus inter-organizational.

The availability of information from a variety of sources was considered particularly relevant to the non-routine users. Non-routine users were those who had the most complex task set and could require multiple technologies to satisfy task needs. Although FINDER shares information inter-organization, there are clear parallels to Goodhue's (1995, 1998) consideration of multiple systems and non-routine information use. By Goodhue's definition, detectives and analysts would be non-routine users; clerks or data entry personnel would be routine users.

Given the distributed nature of FINDER's Query Logs, the number of agencies sharing information can have a direct effect on Query Log reports of system usage. If a FINDER user makes a single query to x number of FINDER agencies, the Query Logs count that as x queries, because each agency is queried. If the number of FINDER agencies sharing information increases, then the value of x queries might increase equivalently, assuming that FINDER users always query all available agencies (FINDER, 2006).

However, it was not known whether FINDER users do, in fact, always query all agencies. The Query Logs did not provide an ability to determine the scope (number of agencies queried) of individual user queries, and casual discussions with users about this topic suggested considerable variance between and within users. Some users indicated that they always query all agencies; some users indicated their query style is contingent on the information being sought in individual cases; and others described expanding, repeated queries until the needed information is found.

The variety of query styles combined with growing numbers of query potentials (the number of FINDER agencies) could skew user activity reports acquired from the Query Logs. The inclusion of a variable to control, at least, the number of agencies available for queries during a given time period was expected to reduce this skew. Thus, the number of agencies available to share information was incorporated as a continuously-measured control variable.

User Workload

The tasks associated with a specified assignment can vary greatly in terms of workload volume (Fyfe et al, 1997; CALEA, 1998). A burglary detective may be assigned 300-400 cases a month; a homicide detective may have a single case a month. Further, a detective in a small agency may investigate all kinds of crime and have the general job assignment of "detective" versus specialized investigative assignments in a larger agency.

The job assignment label does not necessarily reflect workload. Certainly, the same situation exists among workers with similar job titles outside of policing, but no consideration of workload *volume* differences has been found in the general literature. Thus, workload was included in this study for exploratory purposes.

The incorporation of a workload control measure was based on the logic that a user's task-set or related behaviors are influenced by the user's workload. It was believed that a workload influence might be particularly important in the relationship of task-fit indicators (job assignment and FINDER task-fit) to usage rates. In practical terms, a very busy detective might rely more on FINDER (in absolute terms of usage) for assistance than a less-busy detective. Alternatively, a detective who solves 10% of 400 cases assigned every month will potentially have many more chances for "success" than a detective who investigates and solves a much lower number of cases each month.

The job assignment and task-fit variables do not specifically capture task volume, nor is workload identified in Goodhue's (1995) model. However, police literature has recognized that police are inclined to record *activities* (tickets, calls for service, reports) as surrogates for productivity measures (Fyfe et al, 1997). The author's observations supported this; it was expected that FINDER users would have reasonably detailed workload (or caseload) data on hand. The availability of this kind of data was to be established through the user survey.   If workload data were readily available, they could be collected for exploratory analysis in the TTF framework.

User Technology Options and Voluntariness

The final control variable related to whether other information sharing technology was available to the user, and whether the user voluntarily engaged in FINDER use. The TTF model specifies a technology construct as predicting task fit. Technology, in this context, was proposed by Goodhue (1995) as the existence of technology options or the influence of voluntary (versus mandated) technology use. However, Goodhue offered few specifics about the theoretical technology link.

The literature is vague as to the influence of either voluntariness or multiple technology options on user expectations, behavior, or performance. This is a complex issue with little understanding of its dynamics (also see Goodhue, 1998; Goodhue & Thompson, 1995).

When the influences of alternative technologies and voluntariness were considered in this study's design, it was believed that the vast majority of FINDER users were voluntary users. Further, it was believed that no technology similar to FINDER was available, and that there were, therefore, no viable options to FINDER. However, it was recognized that users might believe FINDER to be interchangeable with other systems, and this could affect their use or task-fit perceptions. In addition, it was considered that a user survey could reveal that FINDER users believe FINDER is used most effectively in conjunction with or to complement other systems.

Multiple technologies have been *compared* elsewhere (e.g., Bharati & Chaudhury, 2004), but no research has been found that studies interaction effects in the type of context encountered with FINDER. In a multiple-technology study across different companies, Goodhue & Thompson (1995) employed a *technology weight*. The weight was simply one divided by the number of available technologies. The logic of this method was that the more technologies available, the lower the influence of any one technology. Goodhue and Thompson found that this weight was statistically significant in that particular context but suggested only that the inter-dependence of multiple technologies might be important.

Thus, without clarifying theory or research about this topic, the direct influence of voluntariness or multiple technologies on either

FINDER use or user-level success was dropped from the predictive model suggested by TTF. Two exploratory measures were retained as controls. The first is a dichotomous measure of voluntariness (yes/no). The second was conceptualized as a weighted technology option adapted from Goodhue's (1998) user evaluation instrument and modified to the FINDER context.

Table 4-1: Dependent & Independent Variables in FINDER Study

Variable Name/Type	Variable Type	Description	Source
User-Level Success/ Dependent	Continuous	Number of successes reported by an individual user.	FINDER logs & User Survey
FINDER Task-fit/ Independent	Continuous	Scale value derived from modified TTF instrument. (Goodhue, 1995, 1998; Goodhue & Thompson, 1995)	User survey
Usage Rate/ Dependent & Independent (mediating)	Continuous	Individual user's average number of FINDER queries per day during specified time period.	FINDER logs
Computer Expertise/ Independent	Continuous	Scale value adapted from Goodhue (1995) and Zaworski (2004).	User survey
Job Assignment/ Independent	Categorical	User-reported primary job assignment.	User survey
Training/ Independent	Dichotomous	Yes/No whether user has received training from the FINDER staff.	User survey & PSTC training records

Table 4-2: Control Variables in FINDER Study

Variable Name/Type	Variable Type	Description	Source
Workload	Continuous	User-reported average monthly "workload" or "caseload" volume.	User survey
Agency	Categorical	Name of user's employing police agency.	User survey
Time as LEO	Continuous	Number of years user has been employed as a sworn law enforcement officer	User survey
Time as user/	Continuous	Period of time elapsed between first log-in as FINDER user (measured in days, weeks or months)	User survey
Number of Agencies Sharing Info	Continuous	Number of police agencies sharing information via FINDER	FINDER query logs & User survey
Technology	Categorical (scale or ratio)	Other information sharing technology available to user (i.e., other system name). Alternatively, weighted value of technologies	PSTC & FINDER Query Logs

HYPOTHESES

The primary research question was posed as: *What factors influence user-level success for FINDER's users?* The TTF model and related research suggested that FINDER's user-level success might be *positively* predicted by four variables. These variables were the user's FINDER task-fit measure, the user's FINDER usage rate, the user's computer expertise measure, and the user's receipt of FINDER training. The predicted effect of a fifth variable, the user's job assignment, was non-directional (these variables are defined above in Table 4-1).

A set of initial hypotheses – stated in the alternative form – were proposed to test for the presence of these expected relationships, or influences, on user-level success. They are:

H_1: A FINDER user's task-fit measure will be positively and significantly related to the number of successes reported by that user.

H_2: A FINDER user's usage rate will be positively and significantly related to the number of successes reported by that user.

H_3: A FINDER user's computer expertise measure will be positively and significantly related to the number of successes reported by that user.

H_4: A FINDER user's receipt of FINDER training will be positively and significantly related to the number of successes reported by that user.

H_5: A FINDER user's job assignment will be positively and significantly related to the number of successes reported by that user.

The TTF model and related research also predicted that the FINDER task-fit measure, FINDER training, and computer expertise measure would positively and directly predict usage rate. Job assignment, a categorical variable, was also proposed to have a significant relationship with the usage rate. Additional hypotheses were developed to test for these relationships as well.

H$_6$: A user's FINDER task-fit measure will be positively and significantly related to that user's usage rate.

H$_7$: A user's receipt of FINDER training will be positively and significantly related to that user's usage rate.

H$_8$: A FINDER user's computer expertise measure will be positively and significantly related to that user's usage rate.

H$_9$: A FINDER user's job assignment, a FINDER user's usage rate will be significantly related to that user's.

Figure 4-1 depicts the conceptual relationships of these hypotheses in the TTF framework (the path arrows designate the relevant hypothesis) and sets the stage for collecting data to test the hypotheses.

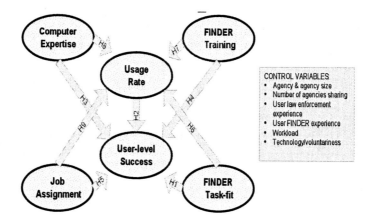

Figure 4-1: Conceptual Relationships of Initial Hypotheses

CHAPTER 5

Sources of Data

The FINDER system presented an attractive environment to test hypotheses about factors that influence user-level success and the specific nature of those user reported successes. The availability of the Query Logs as objective data about system use in combination with the Success Tag reports could be examined alongside responses from a user survey to gain valuable insight to the dynamics and outcomes related to police information sharing.

This chapter provides a detailed description of the data sets that were available at the onset of the FINDER study (the Query Logs and Success Tags). In addition, the *structural* development of the FINDER User Survey is outlined (the next chapter details development of specific survey items). The survey development was based, in part, on preliminary analyses of Query Logs and Success Tags. These preliminary analyses helped identify potential gaps in the data that the survey was intended to bridge.

QUERY LOGS

FINDER's Query Logs capture detailed information about each query made by FINDER's users. Access to the Query Logs was achieved through a police agency computer that had been configured for that purpose. FINDER is available only via Florida's law enforcement intranet and is not accessible to the public (LETTR, 2008).

FINDER connects police agencies via designated computer servers that are referred to as "FINDER nodes." The node permits an agency or agencies to both contribute data to FINDER and retrieve data from other FINDER nodes. The node may provide information-sharing capacity for a single agency or multiple agencies. Multiple agencies can share a node to reduce per-agency costs (LETTR, 2008).

As of April 2006, there were 40 FINDER nodes providing *bi-directional* information sharing among 47 agencies. An additional 15 agencies were known to have "guest accounts." Guest accounts are *not* bi-directional; that is, guest users can query FINDER, but their agencies are not contributing data to the system. Thus, a total of 62 agencies were known to have users making FINDER queries. An additional 59 agencies (for a total of 121) were involved with FINDER, but it was not known what role – if any – those 59 agencies had in terms of query activity (LETTR, 2008). [1]

It is in the FINDER nodes that Query Logs are collected and stored. Each of the nodes records details about each query *into* that node. The nodes do not record information about queries going *out*. Each node stores this information apart from the other nodes. In other words, there is not a central collection point for all FINDER query information. Thus, Query Log data for this study had to be extracted from each of the 40 FINDER nodes. The Query Log data were collected in the following fashion:

1. Each of the 40 FINDER nodes' Query Log files was accessed through a FINDER administrative function.
2. The Query Log files were downloaded to display within the FINDER application. Each node, for each month between December 2004 and February 2006, required a separate download to the FINDER display.
3. Each downloaded was loaded into an Excel spreadsheet. This process created 600 Excel files (40 nodes x 15 months) that reflected a total of 1,836,236 query records.
4. Each of the 1.8 million query records provided the following information:
   a. Internet Protocol (IP) address of the node originating the query
   b. Day of query

---

[1] At any given time, many agencies were in transition from conceptually agreeing to join FINDER, to formally agreeing to join, to actually sharing information. The number and status of involved agencies changed on an almost-daily basis.

    c. Time of query
    d. User name
    e. Type of query (e.g., person, property, vehicle)
    f. Type of query subset (e.g., person/victim, property/pawned, vehicle/towed)
    g. Query parameters (the specific information sought)

5. The Query Log data were organized to identify each user's FINDER usage volume per month from December 2004 to February 2005. During this process, 1,603 user names were identified to provide user-level measurements of the *Usage Rate* and *Time as User* variables. [2]

SUCCESS TAG DATA

Success Tag reports from all FINDER nodes were acquired for the December 2004 to February 2006 period. Each success tag report contained fields for the following information:

1. Report number (automatically populated reference number for the source report or data that is the subject of the success)
2. Report date (automatically populated date of the source report or data that is the subject of the success)
3. User's phone number
4. Report Type (automatically populated type of the source report or data that is subject of success)
5. User's name (not the system user name)
6. User's email address
7. User's comments/description of success
8. Date of success tagging
9. FINDER module used (i.e., pawn, persons, vehicles)
10. Data source (which node provided the "successful" source report or data)

---

[2] Some inconsistencies in node-level query data were noted and are addressed in later discussion of the Query Logs.

A total of 731 success reports, filed by 115 different FINDER users, were collected for the fifteen-month period.

Other PSTC Records

PSTC staff record information, related to the level and timing of FINDER agencies' involvement in the system, was used. One such record incorporates a list of FINDER nodes and the date that the node became active. The PSTC node records were combined with the node-level Query Log data to provide values for the *Number of Agencies Sharing Information* variable.

The PSTC staff also maintained records reflecting the dates and locations of FINDER training sessions. Training records listed eight training sessions conducted throughout Florida, beginning September 2005 and ending February 2006. These records, in combination with related survey items, provided the data necessary for measurement of the *FINDER Training* variable.

SURVEY INSTRUMENT DESIGN

Measurement data for eleven of the twelve study variables were captured either fully or partially through a self-report, web-based FINDER user survey. Clearly, the success of the study hinged on developing and administering a valid and reliable survey that FINDER users would be willing and able to complete. Development of the instrument was approached, first, in terms of general design and layout. This was followed by the construction of individual survey items and pre-testing.

Design, Layout, and Format

Instrument design was accomplished with guidance from subject matter experts, related literature, and instruments used in similar. In particular, Babbie's (1995), Alreck and Settle's (1995) and Dillman's (2000) survey methodology work influenced the instrument's design. In addition, Goodhue's (1995, 1998) TTF, Davis' (1989) TAM, and Venkatesh and Davis' (2000) TAM II instruments were consulted. Finally, Ioimo's (2000) and Zaworski's (2004) TTF police-based surveys helped guide TTF-related adaptations.

The web-based approach was chosen as the sole method of administration (as opposed to paper or interview-based administration) for several reasons. First, and foremost, the identities and physical locations of the user population were not known. This, alone, precluded direct mailing or individually contacting potential respondents. Second, the "blind" distribution of paper surveys to all FINDER agencies was not viable. Such a procedure would have required distributing roughly 8,000 copies of the survey to the agencies (enough copies to distribute to, potentially, each employee of the FINDER member agencies) with the hope that FINDER users would somehow acquire a copy and respond. Third, FINDER users were known users of web-based applications (i.e., FINDER) and would be comfortable with a web-based survey. Respondents' comfort with the survey medium helps produce higher response rates (Babbie, 1995; Dillman, 2000).

A one-page cover letter was composed to introduce the survey and solicit respondents' participation. The cover letter advised potential respondents that completing the survey would be very helpful in developing FINDER to better serve the respondent's information-sharing needs and that a response would help the research team.

The response of all FINDER users was asserted to be valuable, regardless of the respondent's level of FINDER use or affinity. The cover letter also noted that a survey response was estimated to take fewer than ten minutes of the respondent's time. No tangible compensation was provided or offered to respondents. The cover letter addressed Informed Consent requirements and provided contact information for the researcher and UCF's Institutional Review Board.

Respondents were directed to the website where the FINDER online survey was located. The website could be accessed by clicking on a hyperlink contained in the cover letter. Alternatively, directions were provided for cutting-and-pasting the link to an Internet browser if the respondent's computer, network, or firewalls prevented direct access to the survey website.

Upon linking to the web survey, the respondent was asked to log in using his/her FINDER User Name. Each person authorized access to FINDER has a self-assigned user name. It is this User Name that links each user to specific system activity that is tracked through the FINDER Query Logs. However, because of FINDER's distributed technology, there is no central database of FINDER users that directly links the User Name either to an identifiable individual or specific agency. Thus, the User Name login criteria protected against multiple survey responses by one individual and permitted linkage of the user names to their actual system use.

Upon login, the respondent was automatically directed to the first web page containing survey items. The first set of items was intended to be "easy" response items that would apply to all respondents. One key to encouraging respondents to complete a survey is to initially engage them by soliciting responses to items that require minimal mental effort. The first set of questions may be the most important to achieving this (Dillman, 2000). Subsequent survey web pages were designed with a minimum of visual clutter and relatively small groupings of similarly formatted items. The groupings were composed either by the subject matter of the group, the response style (e.g., agree/disagree or multiple choice), or both.

The grouping, or clustering, technique of similar subjects or response styles permits the respondent to focus more on the question asked than the presentation (Alreck & Settle, 1995; Babbie, 1995; Dillman, 2000). These style groupings also permit a minimal use of instructions to the respondent. The cost of mental energy to read lengthy or repeated instructions can cause respondents to quit before the survey is completed (Dillman, 2000).

To avoid bias and error associated with item order (Alreck & Settle, 1995), items were grouped by style and content. These groups were distributed within the instrument with the goal of achieving a balance between consistency of styles and variety of content. This balance was intended to maintain the respondent's interest by avoiding a routine and minimizing the mental effort necessary to differentiate between response modes (e.g., check boxes, agree/disagree, drop-down windows). The FINDER instrument incorporated the liberal use of point-and-click responses and drop-down selections.

The ordering of items *within* the item groups considered cognitive design techniques. Items should be ordered to improve recall by leading the respondent through a sequence of questions that help build an accurate recollection of the desired event (Dillman, 2000). This cognitive and time-referent order of items helps prevent respondent recall error. In addition, within-group ordering incorporated a mix of positively and negatively worded stems. A mix of positive/negative stems helps prevent bias or error caused by a routine of all-positive or all-negative questions (Alreck & Settle, 1995; Dillman, 2000).

The survey items were not numbered. Numbering is unnecessary and potentially distracting in the web format (the items have been formatted and numbered in Appendix A for convenience). Some of the items involved "skips." Skips are branched or contingency questions that, in a paper survey, might appear as: "If you answered 'No' to Question 3, please skip to question 9." In paper instruments, skip questions require careful design to ensure that the respondent understands the directions (Alreck & Settle, 1995; Dillman, 2000). However, the FINDER instrument incorporated "auto-skips" that were performed automatically by the web survey software. These auto-skips were not visible to the respondents. The flowchart in Figure 5-1 depicts the conceptual ordering of item groups.

Graphics and animations were avoided or minimized throughout the instrument. Excessive web graphics distract the respondent from the task of focusing on answering questions. Further, graphics, animations, and sounds consume considerable bandwidth and can cause malfunctions in the survey software for respondents who use dial-up or other low-bandwidth Internet access methods (Dillman, 2000).

In addition, it was anticipated that the survey could take on different appearances between different respondents' computers, computer monitors, and network operating systems. Problems such as misaligned columns and headings, word-wrapping failures, and partial page displays can frustrate the respondent. Thus, the survey cover letter and FINDER instrument were accessed and tested with a variety of e-mail, browser, and hardware configurations to ensure proper presentation and display across disparate network domains.

Response Styles and Scales

The FINDER instrument contained 85 items. The response styles for the items were comprised of:

- 14 dichotomous check boxes
- 7 multiple-choice check boxes (4 nominal & 3 ordinal)
- 5 drop-down selections (3 nominal & 2 ratio)
- 56 agree/disagree (all 7-point Likert scales)
- 3 open-ended text

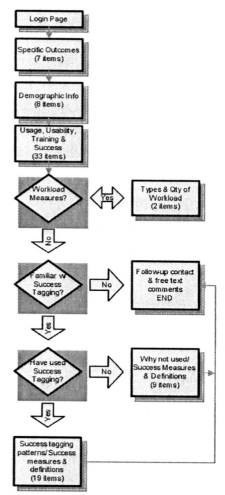

Figure 5-1: FINDER Survey Instrument Conceptual Flowchart

As noted above, some of the items involved skips or branches. Depending on responses to the branched items, respondents were presented with a minimum of 49 items to a maximum of 75 items. The branched items are discussed later in more detail.

The instrument made considerable use of an agree/disagree, 7-point Likert scale. The Likert scale was used because it is powerful and easy for respondents to understand (Alreck & Settle, 1995; Gliem & Gliem, 2003). Babbie (1995) notes the value of Likert-type scales for their "unambiguous ordinality" that reflects the respondent's "relative intensity" of feelings about the topic (p 177). In addition, their agree/disagree formats permit summated values of multiple items that measure attitudes or perceptions about a theorized construct (Gliner and Morgan, 2000).

The 7-point agree/disagree scale is consistently supported by the research literature. The respondent has enough scale-response choices to be reasonably selective but will not be overwhelmed by too many choices, as in a 1 to 10 or 1 to 100 scale (e.g., Cox, 1980; Hasson & Arnetz, 2005). In addition, the 7-point format was reliably employed by both Ioimo (2000) and Zaworski (2004) in the police technology environment.

The scale in the FINDER instrument provided a midpoint choice of "neither agree nor disagree" rather than "neutral," "no opinion," or "undecided." Dillman (2000), particularly, advocates the use of the "neither agree nor disagree" as the midpoint label and suggests that "no opinion," "neutral," or "undecided" labels, where applicable, should be attached to the end (far right side) of the scale.

Initial drafts of the FINDER instrument did not include "not applicable" in the Likert scales. However, pre-testing these initial drafts established that in the absence of a "not applicable" choice, respondents would choose the midpoint value (neither agree nor disagree) – even when the item was not applicable to them – rather than skip the item.

There is a distinct difference, both conceptually and in terms of coding scale values, between neutrality regarding an item versus lack of applicability of that item. Because so little was known about the assignments and interests of FINDER users, it was not possible to design an instrument in which each item could be reasonably assumed to be applicable to every user. Thus, "not applicable" was placed as the end-point selection in the Likert-scaled items.

THE SURVEY ITEMS

Only one of the twelve study variables, the number of FINDER agencies involved in information sharing, was *not* addressed by the survey instrument. Seven variables were measured entirely from survey response; the measures for the remaining four were derived from a combination of survey responses, automated FINDER logs, and various PSTC records (Appendix B shows the relationships between the study variables and specific survey items). The concepts and logic underlying the development of specific survey items are discussed below; the survey items can be seen in Appendix A.

User-level Success

User-level success was the outcome variable of primary interest and, thus, received considerable attention in the survey. The Success Tagging feature was described earlier as the mechanism by which FINDER users reported FINDER-driven outcomes that were perceived as "successes." It was noted that only about 7% of FINDER's known users had reported successes, and that success reports were made in less than .05% of all FINDER queries.

Several possible explanations were offered about the seemingly low rate of reported successes. However, the key issue was whether the reported successes represented *all* successes experienced by FINDER users, or just a *subset* of actual successes. The best pre-survey evidence (focus groups and observations) suggested the latter; that only a portion of actual successes had been reported via the success tagging feature.

The possibility of success under-reporting was believed to be the result of several factors. These included vague definitions of "success;" lack of familiarity with the success tagging function; time lags between FINDER use and the success experience; inconvenience to and time required of the user to complete a success tag; and a perceived lack of user benefit from completing a success tag. With these factors in mind, survey items were constructed to establish whether success tagging data represented *all* successes and, if not, both the degree and causes of under-reporting.

The degree of success under-reporting, if any, was critical to this study (no evidence of success *over*-reporting had been found). Clearly, if this study employed an inaccurate measure of user-level success, it would be difficult to defend any assertion about factors influencing that measure. Therefore, a variety of items was composed with the intent to extract from FINDER users the information needed to compose credible measures of actual user-level success. These measures would be based on a combination of existing data and the survey responses.

To that end, a total of 33 user-success items were incorporated into the survey (six additional success-tagging usability items were incorporated as controls related to FINDER Task Fit indicators). These items were tailored, with considerable overlap, to three success-reporting classes of FINDER users:

1. Users who *were not* familiar with the success tagging function and, thus, had not reported a success;
2. Users who *were* familiar with the success tagging feature but *had not* reported a success; and,
3. Users who *had* reported successes via the success tagging feature.

The survey flow chart in Figure 5-1 depicted item branching between these three classes of users. Thirteen success-related items were addressed to users in all three classes. This included the first seven items of the survey that sought a yes/no response to whether the user had experienced any one of seven common, police success measures (e.g., arrest, case clearance, recovered property). As noted earlier, these seven items were believed to be "easy" responses that would quickly convince respondents that the survey addressed realistic policing outcomes. In addition, if a respondent *other than* the 115 or so who had completed success tags answered "yes" to any of the first seven success measures, the belief that successes had been under-reported would be immediately confirmed.

Five additional success-related items were provided to all users. These items queried user experience in terms of performance gain, efficiency, and user recall as to specific successes. A sixth item initiated the first branch by asking respondents if they were familiar with FINDER success tagging feature. If the answer was "no," the respondent would be skipped to the end of the survey. Respondents who answered "yes" were then asked if they had used the success tagging feature, and the response to this question initiated the second branch of items.

Respondents who were familiar with success tagging but had not used it were automatically skipped to a set of six additional items. These items sought to determine why the respondent had not used success tagging and, if applicable, the level of reported/unreported success. Respondents who *had* used success tagging were automatically skipped to fourteen additional items. Since this class of respondents was known to have reported successes, several items focused on their definitions of success and sought to determine if their successes were under-reported. In addition, the effect of training on their success reporting was addressed, and an exploratory question was asked to get a sense of whether this success-reporting class believed that other users were experiencing successes that were not reported.

FINDER Task-fit

The FINDER study had the advantage over prior research in that a set of individual, actual performance data was available via Success Tagging logs. Thus, the FINDER survey instrument incorporated a tighter focus on task-fit influences that were encompassed by Goodhue's (1995) TTF model. This focus was intended to develop task-fit measures for the users of a specific technology – FINDER – as opposed to Goodhue's approach to technology, generally.

The FINDER Task-Fit items are loosely designed around Goodhue's (1995, 1998) original task-fit dimensions. However, while the FINDER study used TTF as a guiding framework, it is not intended to test or empirically validate Goodhue's work. Thus, only a subset of Goodhue's theorized task-fit dimensions are addressed in the FINDER items. The primary dimensions of interest are usability, ease of use, and usefulness of data. Secondary measurement dimensions are locatability of data, level of detail, accessibility, reliability and the distinction between routine and non-routine use.

The survey items were tailored to respondents in the three success-reporting classes described above. In terms of FINDER task-fit, respondents in all three classes were presented with 13 items. Respondents in the class of users familiar with success tagging, but who had not reported any successes, were branched to an additional four items that related ease-of-use to success. Respondents in the class of users who had reported successes were branched to three additional items that relate ease-of-use to success (the task-fit dimensions addressed by each item are depicted in Appendix B).

Computer Expertise

Technology users who are able to use their computers to complete their job tasks can be considered computer literate (Kim and Keith 1994). Zaworski (2004) operationalized computer literacy in the police information sharing environment as "computer expertise" (p 117) and incorporated related items in his survey instrument. Zaworski's items were borrowed, with minor modification, for the FINDER survey. These three items assessed the respondent's general comfort with learning new computer programs, and whether the respondent is treated as an informal computer trainer or expert by co-workers.

Usage Rate

The single survey item associated with the usage rate variable was exploratory. As noted earlier, objective usage information was extracted from FINDER User Logs. The exploratory item was intended to enable comparison of actual usage rates to the self-reported usage levels.

Job Assignment

The nature of the user's job assignment was captured by several nominal response items (sworn/non-sworn, job title, rank, function). The multi-item approach to job assignment was necessary because nothing was known about the composition of job assignments among FINDER users (other than they worked for police agencies). Absent prior knowledge about job assignments, these items collected task-set indicators from the broad (title) to the dichotomous (sworn/non-sworn). The intent of these items was to develop as narrow a definition of job assignment as the user composition and data permitted. The absence of narrowly-focused task-set or job assignment data has limited the value of prior task-fit research (Goodhue, 1995).

In addition, these items included a search for indicators of the user's mix of routine and non-routine tasks. The information technology needs of users with routine task sets are believed to be different from those with non-routine task-sets. As noted earlier, "non-routine" users are envisioned as having greater analytical (versus administrative) tasks that increase or complicate information sharing needs (Goodhue, 1998; Goodhue & Thompson, 1995; Zaworski, 2004).

Workload

The research model conceptualized the user's workload as a control variable. It was posited that individual workload could influence task-fit, usage, and success independently of the theoretically-predicted effects. Further, it was proposed that law enforcement employees are likely to maintain personal workload records that are relevant to their assignments.

Workload data was sought via three, branched survey items. The first item asked if workload data was maintained; if yes, the second item classified the type of data; and the third item asked the user to estimate monthly workload in terms of the user's workload measure. These items were exploratory.

FINDER Training

The user's completion of FINDER training and the source of training was a "yes/no" item (by possible training sources). An additional agree/disagree item (whether more training is needed) was included for exploratory purposes.

Agency

The TTF model predicts that un-specified "other" user characteristics influence technology use and individual performance. These other characteristics can be related to the user's work environment and normative influences (e.g., Davis, 1989; Dishaw & Strong, 1999; Goodhue, 1995; Goodhue & Thompson, 1995). In addition, police agency size and resources may affect the viability, technological and management support, and user acceptance of technology (e.g., Nunn, 2001). Further, anecdotal evidence indicated that the presence of a FINDER "advocate" in specific agencies may influence user behavior. Thus, four survey items related to the Agency variable sought to identify the name of the user's agency, the type of agency (e.g., police, sheriff, state), and the influence of a FINDER advocate (if any). The agency name (many categories of nominal data) was not anticipated to be suitable to inferential analyses, but agency size could be derived from the agency name.

Time As Law Enforcement Officer

Prior research has found different effects of users' law enforcement experience on their perception of police technology systems (Ioimo,

2000; Zaworski, 2004). This variable was included as a control in the research model. A single item captured the respondents' number of years of law enforcement-related experience.

Time As FINDER User

Existing research contains a variety of findings about the influence of a user's experience (in terms of time as user) on that user's evaluation of and expected performance gains from a specific technology (e.g., Goodhue, 1998; Venkatesh & Davis, 2000). In this study, user experience – or time as a FINDER user – has been modeled as a control variable. Objective, user experience data was available through FINDER's automated Query Logs. A single survey item asked the respondents when they began using FINDER. This item was exploratory (i.e., user recall versus objective data) but also served as a check against the possibility of the user having been a FINDER member under multiple user names.

Technology

It has been previously noted that the user's access to alternative (or competing) technologies can influence that user's perception of the value of any given technology. In this study, the availability of alternate technology was incorporated as a control variable with exploratory potential. Goodhue (1995) included an alternate-technology variable in his expanded TTF model, but noted that the influence of alternate technologies is complex and poorly understood.

Goodhue (1995) accounted for alternate technology simply by counting the number of software applications available to the users in his study. However, this method was applied in just a few homogenous organizations where, plausibly, the count of available technologies was consistent across the user group. The FINDER context was much different since it encompassed more than 120 organizations with disparate technologies. In fact, FINDER was created to help bridge these disparities (LETTR, 2008).

Zaworski (2004) reported that police users (regardless of access to an information sharing system) sought information from a variety of automated sources. The author's experience also suggested that police agencies have a wide variety of stand-alone information systems. These systems serve specific purposes for limited access by specific user groups (e.g., gang database, domestic violence injunctions, and drug intelligence). Thus, alternate technology was conceptualized as *user-specific.*

For example, a gang crimes investigator may not know about nor have access to the domestic violence database. A drug agent may have access to several drug offender databases but not be familiar with a sex crimes database and so forth. Therefore, the survey items related to the availability and value of technologies other than FINDER were specific to the individual user's perception of relevant, technology alternatives.

The five survey items related to alternate technology sought to identify whether the user believed alternate technologies were available; whether the user employed alternate technologies; the value of FINDER relative to alternate technologies; and whether the respondent's FINDER use was voluntary or mandated.

Miscellaneous Items

Three survey items addressed administrative and follow-up issues. One item controlled for the existence of multiple user names by the same respondent, one item asked whether the respondent would be agreeable to follow-up contact by the researcher, and one item permitted open-ended, text comment.

Instrument Pre-testing

First drafts of the FINDER instrument were provided to a review group that was familiar with FINDER and the purpose of this study. A number of suggestions resulted from this review and changes were made to survey layout, instructions, wording, content, and scales. The revised instrument was then presented to ten law enforcement practitioners who were familiar with FINDER but had not had prior exposure to the survey. A paper version was handed to this group with the simple request to "please take it." This group suggested additional revisions; mainly to ensure applicability across sworn and non-sworn FINDER users. In addition, this group reported that the survey could be completed in less than ten minutes.

The suggested revisions were then incorporated into the web-based version of the survey. The online survey was then provided, on a person-by-person basis, to two new groups of five people each.

Members in both groups were familiar with FINDER and the purpose of this study.

The five members of the first group were asked to take the online survey either with the author present or in constant telephone communication as part of a "think-aloud" interview (Dillman, 2000, p. 142). As these five respondents went through the survey, they vocalized their thought about format, style, instructions, and each item. The five members of the second group were asked to take the survey without interruption. Immediately upon completion, they were asked for their perceptions about format, style, instructions, and the clarity or content of the items. This process is believed to have particular value in assessing the ease with which the survey can be taken (Dillman, 2000).

The second pre-test groups offered valuable feedback; particularly with regard to the visual layout of scales and lists of items. In addition, these groups observed that two of the items encompassed multiple topics and suggested that these items be separated into five, distinct items. All recommendations were implemented.

The final pre-test of the instrument was conducted by eight reviewers. Five of these reviewers had no prior experience with either FINDER or the survey. These five reviewers were used primarily as proofreaders. The final three reviewers were FINDER practitioners who had participated in earlier reviews. No significant revisions arose from this final pre-test; the instrument could not be pre-tested with a pilot study because FINDER's distributed architecture prevented sampling users for purposes of a pilot. However, as described above, the FINDER instrument was reviewed and/or pre-tested by more than forty people.

Sampling Plan

The goal of the survey was to gain understanding about the FINDER user population. This was to be accomplished using a sampling technique to study a subset of that population. When the sample is properly constructed, inferences about the larger group (population) can be made based on observations of the smaller sample group. Thus, the sampling technique and characteristics of the sampled group – the group parameters – are critical to assessing the value of subsequent analyses and inferences (Alreck & Settle, 1995; Babbie, 1995; Morgan & Gliner, 2000; Senese, 1997).

In the FINDER study, the units of analysis were the individual FINDER users, and the target population was all FINDER users. The sampling frame was all FINDER users who had used the system between December 2004 and February 2006; this was the period for which Query Logs and Success Tagging reports were available. The selected sample was equivalent to the sampling frame; it included all users of record for the fifteen-month period.   The relationships of population, sampling frame, selected sample and actual sample are depicted in the Sampling Methodology Flowchart of Figure 5-2.   The actual sample results are reported in Chapter 8.

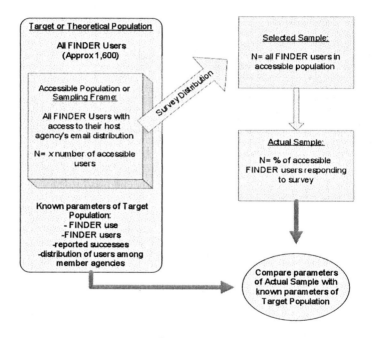

Figure 5-2: Sampling Methodology Flowchart

There were challenges to creating the sampling plan. An analysis of FINDER Query Logs had identified 1,603 user names that had been used for login to FINDER during the period of interest. The Query Logs associate the user name with a FINDER agency via that agency's unique IP (Internet Protocol) Address. [3] Theoretically, these user name and IP associations should have provided a conclusive list of the users and agencies that comprised the target population. However, this was not the case, nor is having problems with sampling lists used in applied research an infrequent occurrence (e.g., Babbie, 1995; Morgan & Gliner, 2000).

Four obstacles affected the ability to accurately define the FINDER target population and its relevant parameters. First, the technology architecture of FINDER places control of FINDER access at the agency level. A FINDER Administrator at each agency determines who will be authorized access to FINDER via that agency's network. Local agency network security processes aside, since FINDER is a web-based technology, anyone with law enforcement clearance, Internet access, and authorization from a FINDER agency's administrator could obtain FINDER access. Thus, responsibility for the composition of the user population rests almost entirely at the local agency level. [4]

Second, FINDER users might share their user name with other law enforcement personnel and a single user name could actually represent many users. Third, users can change their user names. These changes would not be known to anyone but the FINDER Administrator in that user's agency. In this case, multiple user names might actually represent a single user. Fourth, Query Logs are a product of each FINDER agency's local network. If that network has technical problems, the Query Logs can become corrupted. When this happens, the logs might not accurately reflect user and usage activity during the problem period. [5] This fourth obstacle requires amplification.

As noted earlier in this chapter, initial analyses of the Query Logs revealed agency-level inconsistencies in month-to-month query activity. For example, some agencies averaged 20,000 or more queries per month for several months, dropped to 3,000 queries, and then jumped back to 20,000 or more. A look at the Query Logs for the

---

[3] This differs from Success Tag logs which identify the users and their agencies by common name.

[4] Internet access to FINDER is only possible via a police agency's network system (LETTR, 2008).

[5] The interplay of user names, Query Logs, and agency-based system administration emerged during initial Query Log analyses and discussions with FINDER's development team.

fifteen-month study period indicated that anomalous query reports of this type were occurring about 5 to 15% of the time across all FINDER agencies. Discussions with and inquiry by the FINDER development staff revealed that the dramatic variations in reported query activity were due to local system (agency level) corruption of the Query Logs, and there had been no change in query activity. In other words, while about 5% of the Query Logs indicated low levels of query activity in certain agencies at certain times, these reports were erroneous: FINDER use likely continued unabated.

The inquiry into node-level variations in query activity reports provided an example of the interplay between the four obstacles to identifying the FINDER user population. Agency X was interested in FINDER but wanted an opportunity to evaluate it before officially joining the system. Agency Y, already a FINDER member, offered Agency X a "guest account." The guest account permitted members of Agency X to experiment with FINDER via Agency Y's network. In addition, because Agency X was not a member of FINDER, Agency X was provided only a few user names for a trial run. Queries by Agency X guest users appeared in the Query Logs as activity originating in Agency Y. Over a two-month period, Agency Y's network caused corruption of the Query Logs files. This file corruption caused between 50 and 90% of *both* agencies' query data to be lost.

The guest users at Agency X liked FINDER and used it with high frequency. However, officers at Agency X shared user names until their agency formalized participation in FINDER. Once Agency X joined FINDER, some users changed user names while others kept the guest names. Since Agencies X and Y were involved in this host/guest arrangement; none of the other FINDER agencies had any technical or practical need to know about the guest-user agreement. In short, while the Query Logs provide an opportunity for an educated guess about user identification, agency participation, and query activity, there are gaps in the data.

Thus, this example is offered to qualify the reliance on Query Logs to establish the theoretical parameters of FINDER's targeted user population. However, the complexities of guest accounts and query log corruption aside, a review of Query Logs and user behavior (based on the logs) suggested that, in the balance, there were about 1,600 FINDER users for the period of interest. Also, an examination of Query Logs for the period indicated that less than 15% of the Query

Log information showed signs of data corruption. There did not appear to be any data corruption issues with the success tagging logs.

With these qualifications in mind, the parameters of the target population that were relevant to the sampling methodology, for the period of December 2004 through February 2006, were identified as:

- Known FINDER users
- Per-user FINDER activity
- Per-agency FINDER activity
- Distribution of Success Tagging among users and agencies

Two additional population parameters were identified that were not reliant on Query Logs. They were:

- Agency type (police, sheriff, other)
- Agency size

These six parameters were developed to compare against the like parameters of the actual sample: those FINDER users who responded to the user survey. The comparison was planned to help assess representativeness of the sample and the effect of any non-response bias on survey results (Morgan & Gliner, 2000).

Sampling Frame and Selected Sample

It was noted that the sampling frame and the selected sample were equivalent. The FINDER sample was a probability sample in which all known FINDER users had an equal chance of participating in the survey. FINDER users in the accessible population were visible through the Query Logs, but they could not be individually identified or contacted. Rather, it was intended that the accessible population of users would be contacted about the survey through their agency's FINDER administrator. In plain language, "access" to the accessible population relied on forty-seven different agency-level administrators publishing the survey notice to their respective node's FINDER users. Thus, access to users was indirect and dependent on the good-faith efforts of agency-level administrators.

The distribution of the survey instrument was via a website designed exclusively for the FINDER survey. The survey distribution, obstacles to distribution, response rate, and findings are discussed in Chapter 8.

CHAPTER 6

Analyzing System Use

INTRODUCTORY NOTES

In this, and the next three Chapters, a variety of parametric and non-parametric tests was used to analyze data and test hypotheses. These tests, their applicability, and reference sources are detailed in Appendix C. In addition, several conventions were adopted by which both parametric and non-parametric statistics could be described (e.g., "strongly correlated" or "very weakly associated"). These conventions and their sources are also detailed in Appendix C.

This chapter and Chapters 7 and 8 describe, analyze, and discuss the primary datasets and reveal several previously unidentified, alternative measures for User-Level success and System Use. These new measures were included in a final set of study variables used to test hypotheses. Thus, the new or additional variables required that the original hypotheses be modified and expanded. The development and testing of the expanded set of hypotheses are discussed in Chapter 9.

QUERY LOG DATA

Query Log information representing 1.8 million user queries between December 2004 and February 2006 were collected from FINDER's 40 nodes. These Query Log data were collected to construct a measure of "System Use." This measure was initially conceptualized as an individual's rate of use over the 15 month study period (see Chapter 4). However, examination of the Query Logs and the processes by which their data were created compelled the development of *four* measures intended to reflect different dimensions of System Use: Total Queries, Query Volume, User Months, and Months Active. This Chapter describes the data and logic underlying the development of these four measures.

Some important characteristics of the Query Log data that helped frame their analysis include:

- The Query Logs represented activity at the *node* level. A node is a computer server that resides at an agency and provides and receives FINDER information via the Florida Intranet dedicated to the criminal justice system: CJNET. One node can be affiliated with one or several agencies. Agencies could formally share a node or informally permit guest users to access FINDER through the node.

- Each query counted represented a query *received by* a node and did not represent a single query sent by the user. For example, if a user was trying to find a stolen Rolex watch and sent a query about the watch to all 40 nodes, that single query topic (the Rolex) would be counted as 40 queries (one query per node).

- Users' queries of their own nodes were counted in the Query Logs.

- Users affirmatively selected which nodes were queried; the user could query a single node or every node available as a matter of user preference or practicality.

- The Query Logs were maintained at each node's computer server and some node's Query Log files were corrupted. Analysis of the logs suggested that 5.6% did not contain full data during certain months.

- Each node had to authorize access to each of the other available nodes. Users at a given node could not query other nodes until the other nodes were authorized. As of August 2006, twenty-two nodes had not activated full access to all other available nodes. The number of nodes *not* activated (out of forty possible nodes) ranged from one to fifteen.

The Query Log structure created a substantial measurement problem. A valid measure was required to indicate the individual user's frequency of use without over or under-estimating the activity. This problem was compounded by the dynamic changes in agency participation. The number of agencies was not static over the fifteen month observation period. Therefore, a measurement indicator was required that compensated for the Query Log limitations.

STANDARDIZING USERS' QUERY ACTIVITY

Each Query Log event record provided the Internet Protocol (IP) address of the originating node, the day and time the query was received, the user's Username, and the leading query parameters (e.g., name of a person or a type of property). To determine system use rates by individual users, the Query IP and Username were extracted from each query event, for each node, on a monthly basis, for the period of December 2004 (the first month that Query Logs became available) through February 2006. This process identified 1,603 FINDER users[1] who had made queries at any time during the fifteen-month period. Of these users, 253 were eliminated from the analyses because they were administrative, system anomalies (such as an invalid IP address), development, testing, or group accounts. This left valid Query Log data for 1,352 users.

The month-by-month node data was combined and initially sorted to identify, for each user who had queried a node, the following information:

1. The user's query IP address (the user's home node)
2. The user's Username
3. Number of months as a user, calculated from first appearance in the Query Logs through February 2006. A user first appearing in December 2004 would have fifteen months as a user; a user beginning in February 2006 would have one month as a user.
4. Total number of queries per user Dec 2004 – Feb 2006
5. Average number of queries per month as a user

A review of these initial data revealed the influence of the number of available FINDER nodes on users' query volume. In December 2004 there were only twelve FINDER nodes; by February 2006 there were thirty-eight nodes active (and two, inactive nodes). Thus, if in

---

[1] To be precise, 1,603 *user names* which did not necessarily reflect the true number of users.

December 2004 a user had made a single query to all nodes, the Query Logs would have recorded twelve queries. If the same, single query to all FINDER nodes was made in February 2006, the Query Logs would have counted thirty-eight queries.

The effect of the number of FINDER nodes on raw query volume is demonstrated in the example of Table 6-1. User A of the example is a fifteen-month user, having appeared in the Query Logs in December 2004. Comparing User A's raw query volume (Column 1) suggests sporadic, but increasing query frequency over the fifteen month period. However, recalling that query volume is measured by the receiving nodes, the increasing availability of nodes (Column 2) also increases reported query volume even when the user's FINDER use is constant. Thus, when User A's raw query volume is standardized to the number of available nodes by dividing the number of nodes available each month into the raw query volume (Column 3), it appears that User A's FINDER use has been *decreasing* since January 2005.

Table 6-1: User Query Volume Standardization Example

Month	(1) User A (raw query volume)	(2) Number of Nodes Active by Month	(3) User A (raw query volume/ nodes= standardized volume)
Dec-04	258	12	21.5
Jan-05	386	13	29.7
Feb-05	125	14	8.9
Mar-05	312	16	19.5
Apr-05	284	17	16.7
May-05	170	21	8.1
Jun-05	447	24	18.6
Jul-05	370	27	13.7
Aug-05	471	27	17.4
Sep-05	17	30	0.6
Oct-05	303	33	9.2
Nov-05	78	37	2.1
Dec-05	403	38	10.6
Jan-06	136	37	3.6
Feb-06	26	38	0.7
Grand Total	3786	-	180.9

Standardization to control for the increasing number of FINDER nodes would not be necessary if *all* FINDER users were active for the entire study period (December 2004 to February 2006). However, users entered the system at different times during the period, so the raw query data required standardization based on node availability relative to each user's entry. The histogram in Figure 6-1 reflects the staggered user entry during the study period.

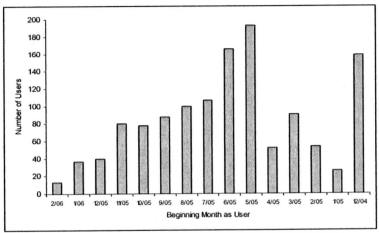

Figure 6-1: Distribution of FINDER Users by Month of System Entry

The standardization convention described above – dividing each user's query volume for each month by the number of available nodes in that month – eliminated the need for the "Number of Agencies Sharing Information" control variable included in the initial research design. Rather, standardized query volume values were used for the balance of this study and produced three, refined System Use measures (a fourth new variable is described shortly). They were defined as the variables:

- User Months: Number of months as a user (calculated from first appearance in the Query Logs through February 2006)
- Query Volume: Average query volume per month as user based on standardized query data

- Total Queries: Total number of standardized queries
made by the user between December 2004 and February
2006

The summary statistics for these three measures are provided in Table
6-2 on page 85.

INFLUENCES ON SYSTEM USE

Query Volume statistics suggested, and a plot of the data confirmed,
positive skew in their distribution. Additional analyses revealed three
influences on this skew that required further investigation: query scope,
repeated queries, and interrupted use. Examination of these influences
provided a deeper understanding of query behavior and was both
conceptually and mathematically important in developing valid system
use measures. These influences are discussed below.

Query scope

Implicit to the logic of standardizing raw system use by the number of
active nodes was the assumption that, on average, users directed
queries to all nodes available to them, or that the increasing availability
of nodes encouraged users to seek information more frequently. In
either case, the increased availability of information was expected to
increase query volume. The Task-Technology Fit model (Goodhue,
1995) supports this logic and suggests that system use is positively
influenced by the availability of additional, useful information.

However, there is little empirical evidence supporting the
relationship between more-information and more-use. Thus, an effort
was made to determine specifically whether FINDER users' *query
scope* (the number of FINDER nodes from which information was
sought) was related to the increased availability of information (i.e.,
more FINDER nodes).

Query scope can be compared to casting a net. Broad query scope
in FINDER casts the net over both a wide geographical area and a wide
set of data sources. Narrow query scope is like dipping a small net in a
fish tank to catch one fish; a small, defined area and target are the
objectives. Query events, or the frequency of queries, are comparable to
each cast or dip of the net.

To understand the query scope employed by FINDER users, a secondary survey was conducted (not to be confused with the primary, "FINDER User" survey outlined in the last Chapter and discussed in depth in Chapter 8). A random sample of ninety users was drawn from respondents to the primary survey that had provided an email address for follow-up inquiries. These users were sent an email request to classify their typical FINDER query behavior in terms of query scope. Eighty-five email addresses were valid; fifty-six (66%) responses were returned. Of those responses, 76.8% reported: "I usually query all available agencies, and then I drill-down in those results to find what I need."

Limitations to the query scope response data were recognized: although randomly selected, the responses were from primary survey respondents who offered their email address for follow-up questions, and who took the time to answer the query scope question. However, their response to the query scope question is decisive with 76.8% of the respondents reporting "query all agencies" behavior.

A number of respondents to the query scope question who reported that they "query all agencies" included comments with their replies. Representative comments (copied and pasted from respondents' emails) include:

- Detective Sergeant: It makes no sense to keep expanding searches when it only takes a couple of minutes for the system to run everything. Especially if you are looking for general information about someone. Which is what I am usually doing if on Finder. However, if I am trying to locate a certain item or person that I know is local, then of course I save the time and just run a local check.
- Detective: Great question, I tried for a while to just look close by but once I know the name of a bad guy I want to know how big his turf is so I will check everywhere. It is amazing how often some people show up.
- Homicide Detective Sergeant: Obviously, in a homicide you query for as much information that you can and then begin the process of paring it down to your specific needs.
- Detective: I usually query all available agencies. I particularly like to read the narratives of prior contacts when they are available. Yesterday, I ran tags from traffic stops on one of numerous tags in a condo community

trying to find an occupied burglary suspect. My third tag gave me my suspect and I await the line up for charges.

- HIDTA Analyst: Actually, I don't drill down once I find a hit, I just use all the information I receive.
- State Attorney's Investigator: I go straight to ALL AGENCIES because I usually have no idea where the information may come from. This has proven to be very useful as there may be several agencies that have info on the same person.
- State Law Enforcement Analyst: The cases I work usually involve individuals that have traveled and/or resided in various counties/cities within the state; thus, I always start my queries with the largest net available before narrowing down the generated output.
- Violent Crimes Detective: I select [query all available agencies]... Data Sharing [FINDER] is the most valuable to tool that I use. It has solved numerous cases for me and my co-workers.

These users suggested that a search for information initially includes all FINDER nodes. This behavior further supported the query volume standardization convention as a more precise reflection of system use within the user's context of *available* information. Conceptually, it is system use relative to available information that is proposed in the task-fit model.

Repeated Queries

As noted above, the Query Logs captures the user's query parameters. Parameters are the topic of the query; the names of people, descriptions of property, and other information of interest to the user. During the collection and sorting of the Query Logs, it was observed that certain users were repeating query topics – evidenced by repeated appearance of the parameters – throughout the month of activity visible in each set of logs. In other words, if a user were searching for "John Smith," the query for John Smith from that user would be seen many times over the month-long Query Log file. In addition, users would sometimes make the same query two or three times throughout a single day.

Repeated query behavior is not surprising. Police information users recognize that new information is always becoming available; a suspect who is not "in the system" today could very well appear in the system at a later time. Lin (2004) documented this practice in his study of detectives' use of an information system. Lin found that police users placed strong value on a "monitoring" system (p. 61) that checked databases repeatedly for newly-arriving information. In addition, FINDER's agency representatives to the Law Enforcement Data Sharing Consortium have called for a monitoring (or subscription) functionality to be built into FINDER (LETTR, 2008).

The FINDER architecture and construction of the Query Logs precluded an empirical measure of repeated queries. However, some understanding of the repeated query influence was desirable. If high levels of system use were associated with high levels of user success, understanding the relationships between scope, volume and repeated queries would be informative.

An exploratory effort was made to determine the prevalence of repeated queries by conducting a detailed examination of ten FINDER users' queries. These ten users were randomly selected from a pool of 110 users who made queries on November 1, 2005. The individual queries made by each of the ten users, for *all* of November 2005, were sorted to check for exact matches in the query parameters. In other words, if User 1 made a query for "John Smith" on November 1st, the data were searched for additional queries on "John Smith" by that user at any other point during all of November 2005. Alternative queries, such as "Jon Smith," "J. Smith," "Smythe," etc. were not matched.

This analysis revealed repeated query behavior among seven of the ten users. The percentage of repeated queries to total queries on a per-user basis ranged from 0% to 50%. Repeat queries accounted for 23% of the total queries by the ten users, and the count of repeated queries was not consistently reflected in total queries (users with high rate of repeated queries were not necessarily the users with highest total queries).

An additional step was taken to gauge the prevalence of repeated queries beyond the limited data shown above. A secondary survey was conducted with a random sample of one-hundred users drawn from respondents to the primary, user survey. These users were sent an email request to classify their typical FINDER query behavior in terms of repeated queries. Ninety-four email addresses were valid; sixty-seven valid (71.3%) responses were returned. The responses are summarized below.

When you make a FINDER query about a person, property, or vehicle and don't get any matching information, do you try the same query again? (n=67)

- Yes, I usually try the query again at a later time. (34%)
- No. If I don't find information the first try I move on to something else (22%).
- It really depends on the case or situation I'm making the query about. (43%)

When you <u>do</u> find it necessary to make repeated queries on the same subject, is it usually because: (n=62)

- I am hoping new information about the subject will become available. (66%)
- Some of the FINDER agencies were "unavailable" on my first try. (26%)
- "Both" or "it depends" [respondent write-in] 8%

These data and responses suggested that repeated queries could have a significant influence on the measure of system use and any analysis of user-level success that is associated with system use. The limited data indicated that a high rate of repeated queries is not necessarily related to a high volume of use. The repeated query rate could be a better predictor of success than volume alone. However, as noted, repeated query data was not available in the FINDER logs, and the effect of repeated queries could only be a matter of speculation relative to its role in system use or user-level success.

Interrupted Use

Query Log data revealed that 975 (77%) of the 1,266 users with at least two months of FINDER activity had months of zero query activity, or "interrupted use." The widespread occurrence of interrupted use was not expected. Figure 6-2 graphically represents the nature of interrupted use among ten, randomly selected users. Shaded months indicate use during that month; un-shaded months indicate zero-query level.

User	Dec-04	Jan-05	Feb-05	Mar-05	Apr-05	May-05	Jun-05	Jul-05	Aug-05	Sep-05	Oct-05	Nov-05	Dec-05	Jan-06	Feb-06
1															
2															
3															
4															
5															
6															
7															
8															
9															
10															

Figure 6-2: Examples of Interrupted Use

As Figure 6-2 suggests, the interruptions appeared random. The interrupted use data was extensively explored in an effort to detect any relationships with other Query Log parameters. The interruptions were not due to Query Log corruption; that would require each node to be completely out of service. An examination was conducted of both the sequence and incidence of interrupted queries by IP address, the month, the timing of first interruption after the start date, the length of interruptions, and query behavior in the month. Comparison of means and correlation tests were conducted for relationships between interrupted use and user months, query volume, and total query volume. None of these efforts identified patterns or relationships that helped explain interrupted use.

The analysis was expanded to consider whether users might have "dropped-out" of FINDER based on their number of consecutive months of zero query activity leading up to February 2006. This possibility was explored through a proposition that users would not return to an active status after two or more consecutive months of no activity. However, a detailed examination of 1,027 users with two or more consecutive months of interrupted activity found that users could take breaks from FINDER of up to twelve months before returning to active use. Thus, no convention for "dropout" could be established.

An understanding of interrupted use was desirable for both mathematical and conceptual reasons. Mathematically, the repeated presence of zero values in the queries prevented construction of moving averages or indices that could have reflected trends in use (zeros in the denominators). Conceptually, interrupted use was important in considering the influence of system use on user-level success. A high level of interrupted use might identify a user who received little value from FINDER. Alternatively, interrupted use might demonstrate excellent task-fit; the user only needed to make a FINDER query to locate very specific, non-routine information. [2]

REJECTING "USAGE RATE": ADDING "ACTIVE MONTHS

Usage Rate was initially conceptualized as a measure reflecting changes in the user's query volume over time. It was hypothesized that a consistent or increasing *rate* of FINDER use over time would be positively related to user-level success. However, the widespread presence of interrupted use precluded the use of moving averages or baseline indices to compute a rate-based measure. Efforts to adapt a trend measure, such as the Cox-Stuart test using midpoint values (Sprent & Smeeton, 2001), also failed. The slope of trendlines, fit to each user's monthly query volume, was computed but was not correlated to any other system use measures. After extensive experimentation with rate and trend statistics, the Query Log data proved unsuitable for the calculation of a meaningful "usage rate." Consequently, the hypothesized relationship of a system use trend was eliminated from empirical tests.

Compensation for the confounding effect of interrupted use and a partial substitute for usage rate was achieved through an alternative measure, and the fourth new variable, "Active Months." Active Months was defined as the number of months a user conducted queries relative to that user's total months visible in the FINDER Query Logs between December 2004 and February 2006. This measure was available only for the 1,266 users who had at least two months as a user (a one-month user could not have interrupted use). Summary statistics for the Active Months measure are presented in Table 6-2.

---

[2] Later interviews with users suggested the latter. Some users employed FINDER sporadically for very specific information tasks.

OUTLIER DATA AND TESTS FOR NORMALITY

Descriptive analyses identified the presence of outlier data in the Query Volume distribution. Outliers can disproportionately influence analyses and should be examined to determine if the outlier data are the result of inaccurate data collection or otherwise anomalous to the research context. However, outlier data should not be eliminated from the analyses unless it is believed to be either inaccurate or misrepresentative of the phenomenon being studied (Gujarati, 2003).

The Query Log data, the source data, were examined for users classified as outliers. Seven were identified based on their averages of more than fifty (standardized) queries per month. No irregularities were observed in the source data for these users.

Four of the outlier users had returned FINDER surveys in which they identified themselves as high-volume users. Three additional outlier users (although they had not returned surveys) were identified as users assigned to a specific detective squad. The members of that squad were all high-volume FINDER users and represented the single greatest source of "success tags" among all FINDER's nodes. [3] Thus, the outlier cases were accepted as accurate measurements and relevant to the study's objectives.

Tests for the normal distribution of the Query Log data were conducted against each variable: User Months, Total Queries, Query Volume, and Active Months. The distributions of each these datasets were estimated to be significantly different from the normal distribution ($p < .000$).

SUMMARY: QUERY LOGS & SYSTEM USE MEASURES

There is little value in conducting refined analyses with source data that is unrefined or inaccurate (e.g., Babbie, 1995). Therefore, the preceding pages in this chapter have described the Query Log source data to provide an appropriate context for their analyses. The objective measures supplied by raw Query Log data offered an excellent

---

[3] While these users were not personally identified, their supervisors and co-workers – who were involved in follow-up interviews – outlined the frequent use of FINDER and high success rate by all members of their detective squad.

opportunity to explore and understand "system use" in the sense offered by the theoretical framework. However, these data must be considered from the perspective of their limitations and un-measured, underlying influences:

- Some FINDER servers were unreliable in reporting system use
- Users may have had FINDER experience prior to December 2004 that is not reported by User Months
- System use measures may be poor indicators of underlying behaviors related to query scope, repeated queries, and interrupted use
- The assumption that, most of the time, FINDER users query all available sources was supported, but not proven
- The existence of repeated query behavior was identified but not measured
- The assumption that volume standardization by node availability is appropriate was supported, but not proven

One objective of this study was to build performance metrics for the FINDER system. The availability of objective system use data, the Query Logs, initially suggested a convenient metric. However, the longitudinal evaluation of the Query Logs highlighted complexities in the data that precluded a single measure. These complexities would have likely gone unnoticed in a cross sectional analysis.

Subject to the expressed limitations, the Query Log data produced measures for four variables related to system use:

- Query Volume: each user's average monthly FINDER use for the period beginning with the user's first appearance in the Query Logs and ending in February 2006, standardized for the number of available FINDER agencies in each month.
- Total Queries: the sum of each user's standardized queries for the entire period of December 2004 to February 2006.
- User Months: the measure of each user's FINDER tenure based on the number of months from the user's first appearance in the Query Logs through February 2006

- Months Active: the percentage of months in which the
  user had query activity compared to total user months
  measured from the first month of the user's appearance in
  the Query Logs and limited to users who were active at
  least two months.

Table 6-2: Summary Descriptive Statistics for Query Log Variables

	N	Mean	Median	Std. Deviation	Minimum	Maximum
All Valid Users between Dec 04 - Feb 06						
Total Queries	1352	45.7	13.0	107.7	0	1615.0
Query Volume	1352	4.888	1.75	9.872	0.00	132.79
User Months	1352	8.560	9.00	3.982	1	15
All Valid Users > 2 or More User Months between Dec 04 - Feb 06						
Query Volume	1266	4.796	1.630	9.922	0.00	132.79
User Months	1266	9.08	9.00	3.574	2	15
Months Active	1266	.563	.545	.333	0.067	1.0

CHAPTER 7

Analyzing Success Tags

"Success Tag" reports used in this study were user-initiated self reports of user-defined successes, arising from their FINDER use. The Success Tag information was highly subjective, with case-specific details submitted in a free-text format, and the Success Tags were not consistently linked to the reporting user's Query Log activity. Consequently, the Success Tag data offered little empirical value. The Success Tag data did, however, help inform interpretation of the Query Logs, the analysis of user survey responses, and guide follow-up interviews with users.

SUCCESS TAG DESCRIPTION, VOLUME, AND DISTRIBUTION

A total of 734 valid Success Tags were identified out of 889 submitted by users between December 1, 2004 and July 30, 2006. The 155 Success Tags that were excluded did not contain enough information to determine the nature of the success. Most of excluded Success Tags appeared to be the result of user error or experimentation with the Success Tag "button" in the FINDER application.

The Success Tag process links the user's self-reported success to a source document provided by a FINDER node. Success Tags included the following data fields:

- The report number provided by the originating agency for the tagged source document.

- The report type classifying the nature of the source document (e.g., traffic citation, pawn ticket, incident report, field contact information).
- The date the source document was made available to the FINDER system.
- The date that the user executed the Success Tag.
- Free-text comments in which the user describes the successful event.
- The name of the police *agency* that provided the source report. Some FINDER nodes encompass several agencies; the data source permits specific follow-up on tagged source information.
- Contact information for the FINDER user making the Success Tag report.

Success Tags were submitted by users in thirty-nine agencies, representing thirty-four FINDER nodes. Eighteen successes could not be linked to a submitting user or agency. The distribution of Success Tags across these agencies was highly skewed. Of these thirty-nine agencies, five were responsible for 80% (585) of all reported successes. Of these top five agencies, two submitted 53% (387) of all Success Tags.

A rough calculation was conducted to determine the rate of Success Tags per node compared to the number of known users per node. Known users were identified via the Query Log analysis through February 2006; Success Tag data extended through July 2006, so the true number of users per node could not be established. This calculation reflected a wide disparity in the ratio of reported successes to known users: the range was 12% to 367%. A figure in excess of 100% means that the number of successes reported at that node exceeded the number of known users at that node (more than one success per known user). When only the top five success reporting *agencies* were considered, the success/users range was 33% to 367% and represented four *nodes*.

The distribution of successes among the 159 users who reported successes was also examined. The top four users, all from the same node, were responsible for 44% (317) of all reported successes; the top 10% of the users (16 users) were responsible for 62% of all reported successes. The range of successes reported per user was from one success (78 users) to 172 successes (one user). The median number of successes was 2.0; the average was 4.5.

Successes were also considered for their distribution in time across the study period. Table 7-1 reflects this distribution. The average number of reported successes per month was 37; the median was 28. November 2005 and July 2006 suggest outlier data at 136 and 110 reported successes during those months, respectively.

Table 7-1: Distribution of Success Tags by Month: Dec 04 – Jul 06

Dec-04	31
Jan-05	15
Feb-05	8
Mar-05	16
Apr-05	10
May-05	12
Jun-05	38
Jul-05	18
Aug-05	17
Sep-05	20
Oct-05	48
Nov-05	136
Dec-05	58
Jan-06	25
Feb-06	30
Mar-06	49
Apr-06	24
May-06	36
Jun-06	34
Jul-06	110

DISTANCE BETWEEN THE SUCCESS AND SOURCE DATA

The Success Tag data provided an opportunity to estimate the geographical or jurisdictional distance between the successful user's agency and the agency that provided the source data. The distance measure was ordinal and specified as:

0 = Data acquired from within user's own agency led to
    success.
1 = Data acquired from another agency within user's county
    led to success.
2 = Data acquired from another agency in an adjoining county
    led to success.
3 = Data acquired from another agency in a non-adjoining
    county led to success.

Of the 734 success reports, the agency location of both the reporting
user and data source could be established in 641 cases. The distribution
of successes based on distance in these cases is shown in Table 7-2.

Table 7-2: Distance Between Successful Users and Source Data

Data Source	Number of Success Reports	Percent of Success Reports
Within user's agency	309	48.2%
Within user's county	239	37.3%
Adjoining county	57	8.9%
Non-adjoining county	36	5.6%
Total	641	100.0%

CLASSIFICATION OF SUCCESSES

Success tag details, derived from the "Comments" portion of the data,
were highly variant in composition and detail. Several depersonalized
examples (copied and pasted from the Success Tags) are provided
below.

- Ref an investigation I was looking for updated info ref
  this subject.
- Capias requested for Burglary, Grand Theft, Violation of
  Pawn Brokers Act. Admission and confession gained
  from suspect, Michael xxxxx. Dollar amount recovered
  was $100.00.
- No arrest, searching one subjects name assisted me in

locating a person that I only had the first name of that is possibly a subject of interest in my case. Investigation on-going for petit theft. 05-xxxxxx

- PROPERTY TAKEN IN BURGLARY ON 11/03/04
- Arrest made/property recovered
- Witness located in drug case for State Attorney's Office. No arrest or property recovered.
- An arrest warrant was obtained for xxxxx for Murder. We only knew his first name at the onset of the investigation but later learned his girlfriend's name. Searching her name provided a report filed listing her boyfriend's full name.

A review of the Success Tag comments suggested a classification convention that was subjective but permitted a rudimentary sorting of the data. The comments were scored across five dimensions and property value. A value of "1" was assigned if the dimension applied; a value of "0" if not. The dimensions are defined in Table 7-3.

Table 7-3: Success Tag Rating Dimensions

Dimension	Criteria
Arrest	Arrest stated, arrest pending, warrant or capias obtained/being obtained
Case Cleared	Case clearance specified without indication of arrest or case cleared with prosecution declined or waived.
Property	Stolen property (other than vehicles) recovered or identified
Vehicle	Stolen vehicle recovered or vehicle of interest identified or located
Investigative Lead	Information acquired without indication of arrest, case clearance, property, or vehicle recovery.
Value	When indicated, value of stolen property recovered or located.

The Arrest and Case Clearance dimensions were mutually exclusive. Investigative Lead was exclusive to all other categories. A property recovery was not assumed to reflect a case clearance. Each comment could receive a score of one in up to three categories (although none did) in addition to a property value. For example, a comment noting an arrest combined with recovery of stolen property and a vehicle with a stated value would be scored positive ("1") for the first three dimensions and include the property value. Based on this subjective scoring convention, all 734 Success Tags were reviewed and scored. The results of that process are reflected in Table 7-4.

Nearly one-third (31.6%) of these Success Tags were different only in their source reports. These tags reflected cases where a single suspect, group of suspects, or investigation was associated with multiple source reports, and a Success Tag was generated for each source report. For example, several cases were observed that reflected identical suspects and case numbers with the only difference in the Success Tags being the Report Number of the associated pawn tickets and incident reports. These multiple-success investigations were the source of outlier data for November 2005 and July 2006.

Table 7-4: Frequency of Success Tag Dimensions in 734 Cases

Success Dimension	Frequency
Arrests	384
Case Clearance	34
Property	537
Vehicle	3
Investigative Lead	142
Property Value	$192,581

INTERVIEWS WITH SUCCESS TAG USERS

Eleven of the FINDER users who had submitted Success Tags were interviewed in person, by telephone, or through e-mail. These users had provided consent for follow-up contact in their responses to the user survey. Included in these eleven interviews were three of the four high-volume Success Taggers. These three, high-volume Success Tag users were responsible for 41% of all tags reported. Each of these users was assigned to a property investigations squad; each of them also was heavily involved in pawnshop investigations. Two of these users were also outlier cases in the Query Volume measure.

These three users described using FINDER as a routine part of their workdays. They ran queries on suspects and property from hundreds of reports that were forwarded to them by other detectives. The query routine was mechanical versus selective or based on a priori hunches or information. One user articulated that he had no "assigned" caseload; he would just adopt cases for which he found information in FINDER and through other sources. Essentially, his case clearance rate was 100% because he only took cases that he had "already solved" through FINDER queries. Each of these investigators identified themselves as "the FINDER person" for his squad or district. Each was also an enthusiastic FINDER member, having been part of the "original" group of detectives who pushed for the formation of the Data Sharing Consortium.

Also interviewed were three Success Tag users who were assigned to analyst positions. One was a pawnshop analyst; one was an intelligence analyst; and one was a crime and intelligence analyst for a state agency. Each had submitted one Success Tag.

The pawnshop analyst described a routine of mechanical FINDER queries based on reports she received from detectives. She related that although she frequently found valuable information in FINDER, she typically forwarded the information to detectives and did not claim a "success." This analyst was also an outlier user in the Query Log data. The intelligence analyst and state analyst described selective use of FINDER that was dependent on specific assignments. The intelligence analyst related that she could go for "a month or two" without using FINDER at all; this was a reflection of her information needs versus disenchantment with the FINDER system. The state analyst thought she would go no longer than a few weeks without using FINDER, and she relied on sworn personnel to make Success Tags on any information she provided.

Of the remaining five Success Tag users interviewed, two were human resources background investigators. They related routine, mechanical FINDER queries based entirely on their applicant workload. A third user was a homicide investigator who labeled herself as the "FINDER person" for her squad and who had made several Success Tags. She noted that when she located "successful" information, she might make the Success Tag, but any case clearances or arrests would be attributed to the detective for whom she had made the query. The homicide detective related that her (and her partner's) FINDER activity was sporadic and based on their need to look for information that was not readily available in their "normal" systems. It was possible for them to go more than a month without accessing the system.

The two final users interviewed were both general crimes investigators from small police departments. Both related that FINDER gave them newfound access to their local Sheriff's data and that this represented a huge step forward in meeting their information sharing needs. In addition, both related that their agencies were unable to afford alternative information resources (such as privately-run databases), and FINDER was their only information source outside of FCIC/NCIC. One detective said he used FINDER almost daily; the other said he might go for "several weeks" without using FINDER because he had a very small caseload.

SUCCESS TAG SUMMARY

The original research plan for this study incorporated a longitudinal analysis that would have examined the relationship of system use to Success Tagging data over a fifteen-month period. However, the analysis of the Success Tag information demonstrated that these success data were too subjective to be used in an empirical analysis. Thus, these data were used primarily to inform the analyses of information from both Query Logs and the user survey.

The unstructured interviews with FINDER users who had completed Success Tags were very informative. These interviews described two types of use that helped explain the Query Log data. The first type of user employed FINDER on a daily basis in a mechanical fashion. This type of use generated high query volume and, in some cases, a very high level of demonstrated success. The high-volume, mechanical users were those associated with property and pawnshop investigations or background investigations.

The second type of user was a more selective and less frequent FINDER user. These users described case-specific needs that arose infrequently; they could have months-long gaps in FINDER use that did not reflect any dissatisfaction with the system. These users included the intelligence and state crime analyst as well as a general crimes detective with a light caseload.

The interviews also revealed an unexpected consideration in the search for an appropriate success metric. Several of these users described being the FINDER source for co-workers who would claim case clearance or arrest credit for those cases aided by FINDER data. In other words, although the interviewed users generated the FINDER successes, the traditional success measures (arrests and case clearances) would not be credited to them.

The user interviews and the Success Tag data also revealed the importance of information sharing within the user's own agency. Several users commented that FINDER gave them access to data in their own agency that they could not acquire through their resident RMS. The examination of "distance" demonstrated the validity of their claim; almost half of the Success Tags employed data from the users' own agencies.

A final point of Success Tag interest was the low number (three) of vehicle-related successes. A homicide detective, who had located a murder suspect through vehicle information, noted that vehicle information was efficiently available through the FCIC and NCIC. FINDER was useful for vehicle information when nothing was known about the vehicle except color and general description, or when a vehicle's association with a person (a non-owner) was of interest. Typically, where a person was identified through vehicle information, that person was the "success;" the vehicle was just the path to the person.

CHAPTER 8

The Survey & Final Variables

The Chapter 6 analysis of Query Log Data provided a set of objectively-measured variables representing various aspects of FINDER System Use by roughly 1,600 users. An improved understanding of the users' context was achieved through the Chapter 7 analysis of Success Tags, interviews, and related follow-up surveys with roughly 100 success-tagging users. To this point, then, this study has identified how often, for how long, and – to some degree – the outcomes associated with individual user's participation in the FINDER information sharing system.

This chapter reports the administration and results of the FINDER User Survey and synthesizes those results with the data, assumptions, and logic developed in the Query Log and Success Tag analyses. The end result is a more thorough understanding of individual user's characteristics, FINDER experiences, and workplace environments that helps establish a final set of study variables. This final set of reliable and valid variables is essential to empirically testing hypotheses about the nature of and path to "User-Level Success."

POWER ANALYSIS

A minimum of eighty-four survey responses was calculated to be necessary to achieve desired statistical power in the analysis of survey results. This minimum sample requirement was identified prior to survey distribution. Ultimately, 402 valid survey responses comprised the final sample and satisfied statistical power needs.

Statistical power relates to the probability of committing Type I and Type II errors. Power, generally, is a function of the significance level, the effect size, and the sample size. If two of these values are known, the third can be determined with a power table. In this study, the significance level was set by convention at p<.05 and, as described below, the effect size was estimated. Thus, adequate sample size could be determined through the power analysis. [§]

[1]   The effect size estimates the degree of influence that the independent variable(s) have on the dependent variable(s). A large effect is more easily detected in a small sample and vice versa (Cohen, 1977; Morgan & Gliner, 2000). Effect size can be estimated by theory, expert opinion, or effect size findings in prior research. In this study, effect size was estimated through an evaluation of prior research. Specifically, the correlation coefficients (r) from prior task-fit and technology-acceptance research were roughly averaged to estimate effect size. Cohen (1977) asserts that this "soft" approach to estimating effect size is valid; no two studies are exactly alike, and r-values are, of themselves, estimates (p. 79). The existing research used to estimate effect size for this study is described in Appendix D.

Prior research reflected a range of approximate effect size from r=.32 to r=.85, or medium to large effect. The lowest effect size estimates were reported by Goodhue (1995) and Goodhue and Thompson (1995). They used an adjusted r-square, which is a more conservative approach in multivariate analyses (e.g., Kachigan, 1991). Their estimate, rounded down to r=.30, was adopted for use in this study as it was the most conservative.

With a known significance level (p<.05) and estimated effect size based on r =.30, the statistical power tables were consulted to establish the sample size required at the ideal power level of .80 (Gliner & Morgan, 2000). The necessary sample sizes for significance testing are n = 68 for directional hypotheses and n = 84 for non-directional hypotheses (Cohen, 1977, pp. 101-102, Table 3.4.1).

REPRESENTATIVENESS OF SAMPLE & BIAS

Notice of the user survey and a request to distribute it to FINDER users was sent by e-mail to all FINDER administrators, beginning May 24,

---

[1] Gliner & Morgan (2000), Kline (2005), and Kraemer & Thiemann (1987) rely on Cohen (1997, 1988) as a primary source in the discussion of statistical power. Thus, while the others offer insight to the power issue, Cohen is cited here as the leading source.

2006. Data did not exist to enable contacting users directly. Initial response to the notice was lackluster; it was determined that more than one-half of the administrators of record were no longer serving in that capacity or did not know they had been designated as their agency's FINDER administrator. An assortment of technology, operational, and management personnel were eventually identified as *de facto* representatives to the Data Sharing Consortium. These representatives were reminded between three and six times each – by a combination of e-mail, telephone, and personal contacts – to provide the survey information to all personnel at their node who had current or past FINDER access.

Of the forty nodes that had formalized their FINDER participation by June 2006, affirmative responses were received from thirty-eight that the survey had been received and would be distributed to users. A total of 430 survey responses were received by August 7, 2006. Of this number, 28 were excluded due to duplications, inability to confirm a valid username, or the respondent's failure to answer any questions. Thus, 402 valid surveys were retained for analysis.

From the pool of 402 survey respondents, 252 were matched with their Query Log data. The remaining 150 respondents were validated as users among a group of 173 new users who were active by June 2006, but for whom detailed Query Log data were not available. Of the 803 FINDER users who were active in the Query Logs by February 2006 or visible as "new" or recently active users by June 2006, the 402 surveys represented a 50.1% response rate.[2]

Several parameters of the respondents were compared against known parameters of the FINDER user population. The purpose of these comparisons was to assess whether those responding to the survey differed in some fashion from those who did not respond. Non-response bias is the biggest threat to the validity of survey research (e.g., Babbie, 1995; Dillman, 2000). The comparisons included response by agency type and size, and the parameters derived from the Query Logs (Query Volume, Months Active, and User Months). The agency size comparison was based on the Consortium's size convention

---

[2] The 402 responses represent 23.6% of the 1,698 usernames that were identified as using FINDER at least one time between December 2004 and June 2006. The response rate cited above is based on users who were active in the six months leading up to the survey.

(LETTR, 2008), and response by node was influenced to an unknown degree by the presence of guest accounts. In some cases, the Query Logs failed to provide information about the user/agency association.

Generally, survey representation was consistent across the agencies by type and size. Statistical testing for differences in representation between the agency and agency size groups was not conducted because the reliability of source data (users per agency) was roughly estimated. Some under-representation was indicated for medium-size Police Departments (between 100 and 249 sworn) and Sheriff's Offices (between 250 and 499 sworn). These groups were comprised of six police and seven Sheriff's agencies.

An assessment was also conducted at the user level for the 252 survey respondents who were matched with Query Log data. The Query Volume, User Months, and Active Months data were compared between the survey respondents (n=252), all non-responding users known to be active in 2006 (n=474), and the population of *all* non-responding known users for whom Query Log data was available (n=1,022).

A comparison of the descriptive statistics for these three groups suggested differences in the enumerated parameters; particularly in Query Volume where the average, median, and standard deviation were higher for the respondents when compared to the full population of non-respondents.

Query Log-based data for all three groups were non-normal but generally passed tests for homogeneity in variance. The t-tests and Mann-Whitney U tests were used, as appropriate to the data set, to statistically test for differences between the groups. The comparison tests found the expected, statistically significant difference between the survey response group and *all* non-responders (n=1,022) in the Query Log parameters. No statistical difference was found in the parameters between survey responders and *active* non-responding users (n=474), except in the User Months parameter.

The difference in User Months was further examined. A comparison of the mean and median values between responders and active non-responders indicated that those responding to the survey had a longer known FINDER tenure. Boxplots of the data confirmed this. The seventy-fifty percentile for responders was fourteen months as opposed to eleven months for non-responders. The interquartile range for responders was seven months compared to six months for non-responders.

The "representativeness" issue in this study is both complicated and enhanced by considering response to the cross-sectional survey in the context of the available longitudinal data. The Query Log parameters were established from data originating as many as twenty months prior to the survey, and there is a complete gap of up to five months (March to August 2006) between Query Logs and the survey. As the analyses of Query Log data reflected, the widespread occurrence of interrupted use and possibility of user dropout complicates assumptions about even defining the difference between a FINDER "user" and a "non-user."

However, the tests of group differences suggest that non-response bias should not affect using survey responses to generalize Query Log data (with the exception of User Months) to users who were active by February 2006. The difference in the User Month distribution among those responding and those who did not indicates that survey respondents, as a group, had a greater length of FINDER tenure than non-responders, at least as of February 2006.

In perspective, however, the evaluation of non-response bias on Query Log data only applies to 252 of the 402 survey respondents. The absence of user-level information attendant to FINDER's structure precluded examining user characteristics for indications of bias beyond what was available in the Query Log data. In the aggregate, 50.1% of all known, active users responded to the survey, and the distribution of responses appears reasonably representative of the user population as distributed by agency type and agency size. Further, the known user-level parameters of survey responders (Query Log data) are, with exception of FINDER tenure, not statistically different from the known user-level parameters of the equivalent (active) non-responding population. Thus, the survey responses in this study were believed to be adequate in both sample size and representativeness of the study population. The use of data acquired through the survey is subject to the limitations noted above.

SURVEY DATA

Eighty-nine items from the user survey were available for empirical analysis. In preparation for item analyses, items were re-coded to exclude "Not Applicable" responses. The Not Applicable option was provided primarily to prevent non-sworn respondents from being scored on topics outside their authority (such as arrests or property recovery). In addition, thirty items had been constructed to evaluate the use of the Success Tagging feature and the reliability of success tags as an empirical user-level success measure. However, the analysis of Success Tag data demonstrated that these data were not suitable for empirical use. These thirty survey items were excluded from further consideration. Thus, fifty-nine survey items remained available for analyses. These items, and the percentage distribution of responses to each item, are presented in Appendix A.

The survey items or their indices were compared to the Query Log data through correlation matrices that were repeatedly updated during the survey analysis. The correlation data provided important information about both expected and unexpected relationships and were used to understand and refine variable measures. In that regard, the first effort toward understanding the survey data required modifying or collapsing nominal data so it could be meaningfully used in the matrices. The first survey items addressed were the nominal measures for agency affiliation and job assignment, job function, and user rank.

Agency

The Agency variable was described as a control for the user's environmental context. Two survey items addressed the respondent's agency name and type (items 8 and 9) and asked the respondent to select the agency name from a drop-down list of all Florida law enforcement agencies.

A total of 393 respondents from 56 different agencies answered these items; nine did not identify their agency.[3] The response total was distributed to 119 (30.3%) from Police Departments, 265 (67.4%) from Sheriff's Offices, and 9 (2.3%) from state agencies. No federal agency users responded. [4]

Of these agencies, forty had fewer than five responses, and nineteen had a single survey response. The range of responses per agency was 1 to 89; the mean was 7.05; the median was 2; and the

---

[3] *Agency*-level responses are different than the *node*-level analysis discussed earlier.

[4] There are no federal agency nodes in FINDER. It is not known whether there were non-responding federal law enforcement employees who could access FINDER through guest accounts.

standard deviation was 12.9 responses. The low level of responses
from some agencies should not be interpreted as a poor response rate;
some small agencies had only a few users. An additional, agency-
context item (item 38) was included in the survey and inquired about
the presence of a FINDER "advocate." This item and its mean score
(1= strongly disagree to 7= strongly agree) was:

Table 8-1: Presence of FINDER Advocate (Survey Item 38)

Item 38		Mean
n=329	I work with someone who is always encouraging me to use FINDER.	3.83

The Agency Type variable remained nominal at three levels:
Police, Sheriff, and State. However, the agency names were not suited
for empirical application (fifty-five dummy variables would have been
required). Both logic and the literature suggested that *size* reflects
differences in the user environment, agency culture, and resources (e.g.,
Fyfe et al, 1997; CALEA, 1998), so a refined agency size measure was
used to represent the agency control variable.

The agency size measure was different than the pseudo-interval
measure supplied by FINDER convention. Those un-equivalent
intervals (0-99, 100-249, 250-499, and more than 500 sworn) were too
broad, and a number of agencies' sworn strength fell at interval
borders. Therefore, the actual number of sworn officers (FDLE, 2006)
in the agencies represented by survey respondents was used as the scale
level measure for agency size. The histogram in Figure 8-1 reflects the
distribution of survey respondents by agency size.

When the Agency Type and re-coded Agency Size measures were
used in a secondary correlation analysis, Agency Size was associated
with change in other items including: users' level of experience,
availability of technology, and job assignment varieties (these
relationships will be explored in later pages). However, no correlations
of interest were found for Agency Type.

Item 38, the FINDER advocate item, was initially intended for use
in the construction of an "advocate" index to reflect agency-specific
norms. However, other advocacy-related items had been dropped due
to the exclusion of Success Tag sections. The use of single, Likert

Scale items is discouraged, so item 38 was not included in the hypothesis-testing models.[5]

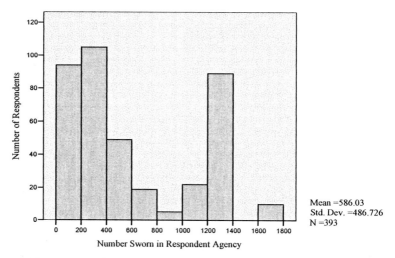

Figure 8-1: Distribution of Survey Respondents by Agency Size

Job Assignment

Job Assignment was identified as a critical variable in the task-fit framework. Four survey items were designed to measure the respondent's task set. These four nominal items (items 11 through 14) asked for the respondent's sworn status, job function, rank, and title.

The rank (item 13) and job title (item 14) responses cannot be summarily described; there were eleven response levels for rank and thirty response levels for job title. Full results on these items are reported in Appendix A. Response to the sworn/non-sworn item (item 11) was 326 (81.5%) sworn and 74 (18.5%) non-sworn among the respondents. Response to the job function item (item 12) reflected

---

[5] Post-hypothesis testing, the effect of item 38 was explored on regression models. The item tested as significant in Model 4 (see Table 9-2) in the prediction of perceived performance and efficiency gains but had no effect in the models of specific outcomes or system use.

assignments of 61 (15.2%) to patrol, 242 (60.2%) to investigations, 40 (10%) to administrative jobs, and 58 (14.4%) to analysis jobs.

The challenge of collapsing job titles into a manageable data set was anticipated. The job function item was included in the survey to help catalog job titles and serve as the four-level default measure for job assignment. The relationships between job function, sworn/non-sworn, title, and rank were examined with lambda (directional) and Cramer's V (symmetric) statistics.

Very strong, statistically significant relationships were identified among the sworn/non-sworn, job function, and job title items. The relationship between those items and rank was moderate. The collective statistical relationships between the items helped guide their re-classification into a manageable set of categories.

First, additional examination of rank data revealed that 78.4% of the respondents reported line-level ranks (i.e., sergeant or supervisor, corporal, or officer/deputy/agent/analyst). Twenty-nine respondents (7.1%) reported higher ranks. Cross-tabulation analyses of the higher ranks with their function and titles (where reported) revealed that twenty-eight of the high-rank respondents were administrators of broad investigative functions. These twenty-eight respondents were, therefore, classified to an "administrative" job title that was expected to be a reliable proxy for rank.

Second, of the forty-seven non-sworn respondents who provided their job title, forty-two (89.4%) identified themselves as analysts. Thus, the analyst title or job classification was expected to serve as a reliable proxy for the respondent's sworn status.

Third, specific job titles were reported by 341 (85%) of the respondents while job function was reported by all but one respondent. Guided by the both users' reports of job function relative to job title and the classifications suggested by the statistical tests, a set of seven job functions was created. These seven functions, and their distribution among survey respondents, are shown in Table 8-2.

The frequency of patrol and analytical job assignments – comprising 26% of the responding users – was higher than expected. The prevalence of property investigators as the largest group of users was expected due to FINDER's property-based origins.

Table 8-2: Variables for Job Assignment Measure

Variable	Frequency	Percent
Patrol	64	16.0%
All Investigations	48	12.0%
Property Investigations	121	30.3%
Persons Investigations	32	8.0%
Other Investigations	33	8.3%
Analysis	43	10.8%
Admin/Other	61	15.1%
Total	402	100.0%

User-Level Success

The survey included twelve items designed to measure dimensions of user-level success. These dimensions included specific outcomes, perceived changes in user performance, and perceived changes in user efficiency. Items one through seven captured specific outcome information. Those items and their results are shown in Table 8-3.

Table 8-3: Items Comprising User-level Success Index

Have you:		Yes	Yes%	No	No%
1.	Made an arrest?	148	45.7%	176	54.3%
2.	Solved a case?	172	51.8%	160	48.2%
3.	Recovered property?	140	43.9%	179	56.1%
4.	Identified a suspect?	217	63.6%	124	36.4%
5.	Located a person?	203	60.2%	134	39.8%
6.	Recovered a vehicle?	14	4.8%	275	95.2%
7.	Discovered a crime?	91	29.1%	222	70.9%

Five additional items were related to changes in user performance and efficiency. These items and their mean scores (1= strongly disagree to 7= strongly agree) are reflected in Table 8-4.

These twelve success and performance items, together, were examined through a correlation analysis (Cramer's V). As expected, with the exception of "recovered a vehicle" (item 6), all items strongly or very strongly correlated at p<.001. Item 6 ('vehicle') was weakly correlated at p<.05 with some items and not significantly correlated with other items.

Table 8-4: Items Comprising Performance/ Efficiency Index

Item		Mean
28	FINDER has helped me improve my job performance. n=355	5.28
36	FINDER has helped me solve or prevent crimes. n=306	4.93
45	It is easy for me to give specific examples of how FINDER has helped me do my job. n=346	4.69
21	FINDER helps me do my job more efficiently. n=356	5.64
42	FINDER saves me a lot of time. n=357	4.86

The twelve items described above reflect the theoretically and logically supported construct of "user-level success" across distinct dimensions. Items 1 through 7 are dichotomous (yes/no) measures of specific *outcomes*. Items 28, 36, 45, 21, and 42 are scaled items of performance *perceptions*. The scale and conceptual differences between the two sets of items prevented their combination into a combined measure. Thus, they will be discussed separately.

Items 1 through 7 were identified as the best measure of the *level* of user-level success although it provides no measure of frequency in the items. The use of these items for the success measure required that they reflect the success construct in both a reliable and valid manner. Reliability refers to the consistency of the items, taken together, in representing the idea of success. In other words, the measure of each item (yes/no) relative to the others should remain consistent among users who report similar levels of success.

Reliability of items 1 through 7 was tested with the Cronbach's Alpha statistic. An Alpha value greater than .70 indicates acceptable reliability; greater than .80 is good or very good; values approaching or exceeding .90 are excellent in terms of indicating reliability among the items (Gliem & Gliem, 2003; Gliner & Morgan, 2000; Kline, 2005). The initial Alpha value was good, but improvement in reliability was predicted with the removal of item 6 ("recovered a vehicle"). With item 6 removed, the Alpha value for the remaining six items was .882, indicating very good reliability.

The validity of the items as a success measure was also considered. The removal of item six was supported statistically and through evidence offered by the review of the Success Tag data. The Success Tags had very few reports of vehicle "successes," and a user had suggested that "vehicle recoveries" were typically achieved through systems like the NCIC. The validity of the remaining six items in a success measure was supported by the task-fit framework and prior research and literature (e.g., BJA, 2005; Zaworski, 2004).

The remaining six success items required transformation to a single measure, an index, to be suitable for hypothesis testing (e.g., Babbie, 1995). A summative index, adding-up responses where "Yes" = 1 and "No" = 0 was not feasible because some of the items were not applicable to some users (e.g., non-sworn users can't make arrests). Thus, the measure had to reflect the success level relative to each user's success capacity. This was achieved by measuring success as the ratio (percentage) of reported successful outcomes to successful outcomes possible per respondent (excluding "Not Applicable" responses). This ratio, the Success Index, provided a scale measure (0.0 to 1.00) that represented the level of success reported by the survey respondent.

The histogram in Figure 8-2 illustrates the distribution of the Success Index values among the respondents. The mean index value was .4495, and the median index value was .330 with a standard deviation of .393. These statistics indicate that, on average, users experienced success in about one-half (44.95%) of the dimensions applicable to them, and half of the survey respondents experienced success in less than one-third (33.0%) of the applicable dimensions. Of the 402 respondents, 83 (20.6%) reported 100% success across applicable items, and 127 users (31.6%) reported no success.

Items 28, 36, 45, 21, and 42 report users' perceptions about changes in their performance and task efficiency attributed to FINDER. These items were all very strongly associated with rho values ranging from 0.535 to 0.707 and p<.001 in all relationships. The strength of these relationships indicated that these five items represented a performance and efficiency construct within the general concept of user-level success. The items were tested for reliability, using Cronbach's Alpha, in the same fashion as items 1 through 7. The Alpha value for the five items was .876, indicating very good reliability in their measurement of the construct. No improvement in the Alpha value was accomplished by eliminating any of the items.

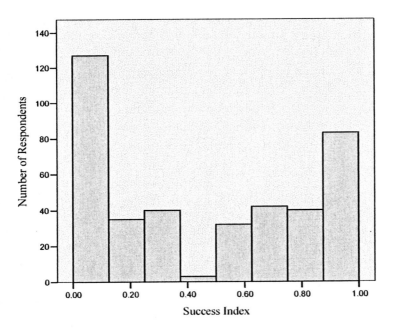

Figure 8-2: Distribution of Success Index Values in Survey Responses

These five items were also evaluated for their validity in representing a construct of performance and efficiency. All of the items are well-grounded in the Task-technology Fit model (Goodhue,

1995) and in parallel items validated in Zaworski's (2004) study of police information sharing. Consequently, these items were considered to be reliable and valid indicators of FINDER users' perceptions of changes in individual performance and efficiency attributed to their FINDER use.

Since items 28, 36, 45, 21, and 42 were identically scaled and conceptually similar (on a seven-point, agree/disagree scale), they were suitable for inclusion in an index (e.g., Babbie, 1995). The index value was created for each user by averaging that user's response across the items. This index was labeled the Performance/Efficiency Index.[6] As expected, this index was strongly correlated to the User-level Success measure ($r= 0.661$, $p< .001$). The strength of this correlation indicates that users' perceptions about increases in individual performance and efficiency are highly related to their level of successful outcomes.

The Success Index was conceptualized to be a subset of the Performance/Efficiency Index. The Success Index measures outcomes; the Performance/Efficiency Index measures general performance perceptions that (at a minimum) include successful outcomes and efficiency. This suggests that combining the two is "double counting." Therefore, the two indices were considered mutually exclusive as dependent variables and would require separate models to test for user-level success.

Frequency of use

Item 19 was the single item used to measure respondents' frequency of FINDER use. The item and its results are shown in Table 8-5. It was unexpected that a significant number of survey respondents would be new users or users not visible in the Query Logs. Thus, the frequency of use measure acquired from item 19 was the only system use measure available for 150 (37%) of those responding to the survey.

The responses to item 19 were compared to the objective data from the Query Logs to help determine whether they were similar measures. Item 19 was significantly ($p<.01$) and positively correlated to Total

---

[6] A Confirmatory Factor Analysis model was tested to fit these items to separate constructs of Performance and Efficiency. The data did not fit the model.

Table 8-5: Frequency of FINDER Use (Survey Item 19)

19. How often do you use FINDER?		
	Frequency	Percent
Almost never	91	22.9%
Few times a month	122	30.7%
About once a week	37	9.3%
Few times a week	68	17.1%
Almost every day	80	20.1%
Total	398	100.0%

Queries (r=.468), Query Volume (r=.473), and Active Months (r=.604). Further, item 19 was positively and significantly correlated (p<.01) to both the Success Index (r=.616) and the Performance/Efficiency Index (r=.637). These moderate or strong correlations suggested that item 19 offered an alternative system use measure to the objective data; particularly with regard to the Active Months measure.

The Query Log data were manipulated to determine if a composite measure would gain associational value with item 19. Several combinations were tried, but the product of Active Months and Total Queries achieved the best correlation value with item 19 responses (r=.462, p<.01), which was less than the r value of item 19 to Active Months (r=.604). Conceptually, item 19 was a better representation of Active Months (frequency) versus volume (Total Queries and Query Volume) and appeared to represent a viable proxy to the Active Months measure.

FINDER Task-fit

The FINDER Task-fit variable was conceptualized along theory and research-based dimensions of system usefulness and usability. These dimensions were measured through fifteen survey items that were expected to provide a measure of the FINDER Task-fit construct. The fifteen items are presented in two groups. The first group (items 30, 31, and 34) was excluded from the FINDER Task-fit Index discussed below and is shown in Table 8-6.

Table 8-6: Items Excluded from FINDER Task-fit Index

		Mean
30	I use FINDER to search for property more than I use it to search for people. n=338	4.48
31	In my job I have to use multiple computer systems to assemble the information I need. n=376	5.47
34	I only use FINDER if I am looking for a person or property outside of my jurisdiction. n=357	3.53

The second group of twelve items was used to construct the index shown in Table 8-7. The items and their mean scores (1= strongly disagree to 7= strongly agree) are reported in the Tables.

Reliability testing used Cronbach's Alpha and produced an initial Alpha value of .715, or an acceptable level of reliability for all fifteen items. The Cronbach's Alpha test suggested that reliability could be improved by dropping some of the items. Two of these items, 30 and 34, addressed specific FINDER search behaviors versus usefulness or

Table 8-7: Items Comprising FINDER Task-fit Index (Cronbach's Alpha = .824)

		Mean
22	FINDER is easy to use. n=374	5.82
23	I use FINDER only as a last resort. n=354	2.56
25	I use FINDER to locate information about people. n=360	5.78
27	FINDER provides me information that I cannot get from any other source. n=361	5.33
29	FINDER has helped me locate people that I couldn't find through other techniques. n=349	4.91
33	Most of the time, FINDER provides information that is useful to me. n=362	5.43

Table 8-7 (continued): Items Comprising FINDER Task-fit Index

35	I use FINDER's "Link Analysis" to get the information I need. n=309	4.40
37	I have to make a lot of queries on FINDER to get the information I need. n=350	3.63
40	I would use FINDER more often if it did not take so long to get a response to my queries. n=354	3.70
43	I think FINDER is poorly designed. n=364	2.76
47	FINDER would be more useful to me if it had analytical tools. n=349	4.11
48	The best thing about FINDER is I can get information that I was not able to get before. n=359	5.35

usability. These two items were logically justified for being excluded from the task-fit index. A third item, 31, asked about the availability of systems other than FINDER. This item, on its face, reflects a different concept than usefulness or usability, and also was dropped from the task-fit index.[7]

The remaining twelve items were re-tested using Cronbach's Alpha and produced an Alpha statistic of .824. This Alpha value suggests a good level of reliability among the items. No significant increase in the reliability coefficient would have been achieved by eliminating additional items.

Since all twelve items were identically scaled and conceptually similar (on a seven-point, agree/disagree scale), they were suitable for inclusion in an index (e.g., Babbie, 1995). The index value was created for each user by averaging that user's response across the items. Five of the items (23, 37, 40, 43, and 47) had been reverse coded because they were negatively worded; their mean values were adjusted accordingly. The resulting index value was used as the measure for the FINDER Task-fit variable.

---

[7] Item 31 was later considered for suitability as a component of the Technology construct.

Computer expertise

The Computer Expertise variable was conceptualized through theory and research that suggested a FINDER user's level of computer expertise would positively influence that user's level of success. Computer expertise was to be measured by three survey items (26, 32, and 39). The reliability and validity of these items in their representation of Computer Expertise is discussed below. These three items and their mean scores (1= strongly disagree to 7= strongly agree) are reported in Table 8-8.

Reliability testing of the items was conducted using Cronbach's Alpha and produced an Alpha value of .760, or an acceptable level of reliability. However, the Cronbach's Alpha analysis indicated that reliability would be increased to .842 (good or very good reliability) if item 26 were dropped.

Table 8-8: Items Comprising Computer Expertise Index (Cronbach's Alpha = .760)

		Mean
26	I am usually comfortable with learning new computer programs. n=379	5.88
32	My co-workers often ask me to help them with computer problems. n=368	5.01
39	My co-workers often ask me to help teach them how to use software. n=353	4.53

The Cronbach's Alpha analysis suggested the presence of a different dimension being measured by item 26 when compared to items 32 and 39. While item 26 deals exclusively with the user's level of comfort (or computer expertise) with new programs, items 32 and 39 expand computer expertise to the dimension of helping co-workers. In other words, the concept of measuring any one user's level of "computer expertise" is diluted in items 32 and 39 by also measuring that user's status (or willingness) as the go-to computer person for co-workers.

The mix of helping co-workers and computer expertise is not specifically validated within the task-fit framework employed by this study. Zaworski (2004, pp. 116-117) found no significant relationship between "assists co-workers with computer problems" and "computer knowledge," but he did not otherwise test the items.

The question in terms of the User Expertise construct was whether to accept the three-item construct (with an adequate reliability coefficient); drop item 26 to increase reliability (but lose the user's self-assessment of expertise); or employ a single item (item 26) as the User Expertise measure. The decision was made to use the three-item index. This decision was justified for two reasons. First, there are statistical risks associated with use of Likert-scaled, single-item measures (e.g., Gliem & Gliem, 2003). Second, a user's willingness to assist others may be important to this study (see the earlier discussion about squad-level FINDER experts). Further, and by definition, "expertise" is a relative term of perceived ability between people that is independent of the "expert's" self-assessment.

Since the three items were identically scaled and conceptually similar, they were suitable for inclusion in an index. The Computer Expertise index value was created for each user by averaging that user's response across the three items. Any interpretation of this index's influence on User-Level Success or System Use must recognize that "computer expertise" captures both the user's self-assessment of skill and that user's status as a computer "expert" within his or her work environment.

Workload

The Workload variable was conceptualized through theory and research that suggested a FINDER user's workload would be useful as a control for that user's level of system use. Workload was to be measured by a single survey item (item 52). This item was answered in a three-step process that first identified whether the respondent tracked workload and then the respondent's type of workload and finally asked the respondent to characterize monthly workload in approximate intervals.

Of 402 respondents, 330 reported a workload measure. The item and the frequency of responses are shown in Table 8-9.

Table 8-9: Workload Measure (Survey Item 52)

Item 52. On average, how many [calls, cases, projects, meetings] do you handle each month?		
	Frequency	Percent
Fewer than 10	28	8.5
Between 10 and 50	185	56.1
Between 51 and 100	76	23.0
More than 100	41	12.4
Total Responses	330	100.0

The workload item responses were reviewed in correlation and covariance analyses. No significant relationships were found between workload and the other variables or items of interest. The correlation coefficient for workload compared to Query Volume, Total Queries, Agency Size, Success, Success Tags, and Job Assignment were less than $r=0.10$ and not statistically significant. It is noted that no conceptual argument is made that "between 10 and 50" cases is a workload equivalent to "between 10 and 50" projects or any other workload type. The workload item was exploratory.

Training

The Training variable was conceptualized through theory and research that suggested users who had received FINDER training would be more successful than those who had not. Two survey items were designed to build a measure of each user's level of FINDER training. The first (item 20) related to types of training received; the second (item 46) considered the user's perceived need for additional training. The items and responses are detailed in Tables 8-10 and 8-11.

The training received item (20) was re-coded into four dummy variables: no training, co-worker/supervisor training, agency training, and UCF training. Of the three training types, the UCF training was the only type to have an established curriculum that would have been presented in a consistent fashion, regardless of the respondent's agency affiliation.

Table 8-10: FINDER Training Received (Survey Item 20)

20. What kind of FINDER training have you received?	Frequency	Percent
Co-worker or supervisor, UCF, and agency training	3	0.8%
Co-worker or supervisor and UCF training	10	2.5%
Co-worker or supervisor and agency training	10	2.5%
Agency training and UCF training	7	1.8%
Co-worker or supervisor training only	150	38.1%
UCF training only	35	8.9%
Agency training only	56	14.2%
No training	123	31.2%
Total	394	100.0%

Table 8-11: Value of FINDER Training (Survey Item 46)

Item 46 (1 to 7 agree/disagree scale)	Mean
I could get better results from FINDER if I were provided more training about how to use it. n=361	4.10

The responses to item 46 (need more training) were checked for relationships to the training variables. Cramer's V (nominal to nominal) and Spearman rank (ordinal to ordinal) methods found item 46 significantly and negatively related to the UCF training variable and positively related to the No Training variable. The relationships to co-worker/supervisor and agency training were negative but not statistically significant. These relationships indicated that item 46 accurately reflected the intent of the question.

In terms of users' satisfaction with training received, the strongest relationship (more satisfied) was with the formalized UCF/FINDER curriculum, and the least satisfaction was associated with no training at all.

The four dichotomous training variables (training dummies) were retained for empirical testing. Item 46 was cautiously retained with recognition that the use of a single, Likert-scale item poses measurement risks (e.g., Gliem & Gliem, 2003).

Law Enforcement Experience and FINDER Experience

Both law enforcement experience and Time as FINDER User were proposed in the research framework as controlling for the user's law enforcement and FINDER experience against other factors influencing user-level success. They are both discussed here.

Law enforcement experience was measured by a single item (item 15) that reflected from less than one year of experience to more than twenty years of experience. The mean number of years of experience was 13.27 years; the median years of experience was 14 years; and the standard deviation of the years of experience distribution was 5.78. The mode of the distribution was 20 years or more of experience; this group represented 25% of all respondents.

FINDER experience was computed from the Query Logs as User Months (when the survey respondent was matched with query data). It is important to note that User Months were calculated only for the 252 respondents who were visible in the Query Logs between December 2004 and February 2006.

Item 16 asked respondents to report when they first began using FINDER. These responses were not usable. Nearly half of the respondents failed to recall either the year or month (or either) that started their FINDER use. For those respondents who did complete the item and whose answer could be checked with Query Log data, the self-report data was generally inaccurate. Consequently, the User Months data was the only reliable data available to represent FINDER experience, and it was limited to 252 (63%) of the respondents. These data were discussed in the Query Log analysis in Chapter 6.

The senior status of many respondents (twenty-five percent with twenty or more years of service) was not expected. Correlation analysis indicated that years of law enforcement experience was weakly, but significantly, correlated with agency size, Sheriff's Offices, User Months, and "other" investigative positions. The strongest correlation ($r=.204$, $p<.01$) was with User Months. This suggested a relationship between FINDER and general law enforcement seniority.

The failure of item 16 to accurately report respondents' time in the FINDER system was not unexpected. The potential for respondent recall problems was anticipated. The risk of relying on self-report recall information was verified by the ability to compare the recall responses to the objective data from the Query Logs.

Technology

Goodhue's (1995) Task-technology Fit model and subsequent research suggest that competing technologies and voluntariness of use have some unknown degree of impact on the use of the system being studied. If users are required to use a particular technology, then system use could be inflated, regardless of the system's value to the user. If the user has multiple technology options, then system use can be diluted in the system being studied. The Technology construct of this study was intended to measure both the voluntariness and technology-option dimensions.

Voluntariness was addressed by a single item (item 17) asking the respondents whether they were required to use FINDER. Of the 402 responses, 352 (87.6%) said "no," and 46 (11.4%) answered "yes."

Technology options were to be measured by three items (31, 44, and 49). The initial reliability test of the three items produced a Cronbach's Alpha value of .462 that indicated that the three items did not provide a reliable measure of the Technology construct. When item 31 was dropped ("In my job I have to use multiple computer systems to assemble the information I need"), the Alpha value increased to .648 for items 44 and 49. These two items and their mean scores (1= strongly disagree to 7= strongly agree) are shown in Table 8-12.

Responses to item 17 reflected that the great majority (87.6%) of respondents' FINDER use was voluntary. This was important because Goodhue (1995) posited that non-voluntary system use would complicate any analyses of the effect of system use on individual performance (user-level success). The presence of some non-voluntary users in the response group permitted a statistical assessment of this effect.

The relatively low Cronbach's Alpha of .648 for the two technology options items (44 and 49) could not be explained. The questions were, essentially, mirror images, and were posed in both the positive and negative context to protect against response bias.

Table 8-12: Items Comprising Technology Index
(Cronbach's Alpha = .648)

		Mean
44	I have computer tools other than FINDER to help me get information from outside of my jurisdiction. n=370	4.41
49	FINDER is the only computer tool I have to get information from other police agencies. n=369	3.90

Responses to these two items were reviewed, case-by-case, to check for coding errors; none were found (Dillman, 2000). An examination of correlations between the two items and other items and indices was also conducted.

The items were identical in terms of significant correlations, but item 44 had slightly stronger correlation values with other items and constructs of interest. It is possible that responses to item 49 were biased because of its close proximity to item 44 ('routine' bias) or because it was the last in the series of twenty-nine agree/disagree items ('fatigue' bias).

In the initial development of variables for this study, the Technology variable was identified as exploratory. The use of items with Cronbach's Alpha values less than .70 and as low as .50 has been supported when the items represent exploratory concepts (Hair et al, 1998; McMillan & Schumacher, 1993). Thus, response to items 44 and 49 were averaged and adopted as a measure of Technology (alternative technologies).

FINAL STUDY VARIABLES

The initial and final variables derived from the Query Logs and the user survey, and informed by the Success Tag analysis, are presented in Table 8-13.

Table 8-13: Final Study Variables				
Initial Variable (Name/Type)	Final Measures	Level	Description	Source
User-Level Success/ Dependent		Scale	Number of successes reported by an individual user.	FINDER logs & User Survey
	Success Index	Scale	Percentage of six, applicable, successful outcomes reported by users.	Survey Items 1-5, & 7
	Performance/ Efficiency Index	Scale	Average of five, 7-point scale items.	Survey Items 21, 28, 36, 42, & 45
Usage Rate/ Dependent & Independent (mediating)		Scale	Individual user's average number of FINDER queries per day during specified time.	FINDER Query Logs
	Total Queries	Scale	Total FINDER queries by user between Dec 04 & Feb 06. Weighted by number of available FINDER nodes by month.	FINDER Query Logs
	Query Volume*	Scale	User's average FINDER queries per month following user's first appearance in Query Logs. Standardized by available FINDER nodes by month.	FINDER Query Logs
Usage Rate/ Dependent & Independent (continued)	Active Months	Scale	Percentage of User Months with query activity after user's first appearance in Query Logs (active mos. /total mos. In FINDER) between Dec 04 & Feb 06.	FINDER Query Logs
	Frequency of Use	Ord-inal	Approximate-interval scale of user's frequency of use during month or week.	User Survey item 19

121

Initial Variable (Name/Type)	Final Measures	Level	Description	Source
FINDER Task-fit/ Independent		Scale	Scale value derived from modified TTF instrument. (Goodhue, 1995, 1998)	User survey
	FINDER Task-fit Index	Scale	Average of twelve, 7-point scale items measuring FINDER usefulness & usability.	User survey items 22, 23, 25, 27, 29, 33, 35, 37, 40, 43, 47,48
Computer Expertise/ Independent		Scale	Scale value derived from adapted from Goodhue (1995) and Zaworski (2004).	User survey
	Computer Expertise Index	Scale	Average of three, 7-point scale items. (Exploratory variable)	User survey items 26, 32, & 39
Job Assignment/ Independent		Nom-inal	User-reported primary job assignment.	User survey
	Primary Job Function	Nom-inal	Patrol, Investigations, Analysis/Support, Administrative (4 categories)	User survey item 12
	Job Title*	Nom-inal	Patrol, All Investigations, Property Investigations, Persons Investigations, Other Investigations, Analysis, Other (seven categories)	User survey items 12 & 14
	Sworn Status*	Nom-inal	Sworn or non-sworn status	User survey item 11
Workload/ Control		Scale	User-reported average monthly "workload" or "caseload" volume.	User survey
	Average Monthly Workload	Ord-inal	Approximate interval measure of average number of user-relevant workload events per month. (Exploratory)	User Survey item 52

Table 8-13: Final Study Variables (continued)

Initial Variable (Name/Type)	Final Measures	Level	Description	Source
Training/ Independent		Nom-inal	Yes/No whether user has received training from the FINDER staff.	User survey & PSTC records
	Training Yes/No*	Nom-inal	Whether user reports receiving any type of FINDER training.	User survey item 20
Training/ Independent (continued)	FINDER Training Yes/No	Nom-inal	Whether user reports receiving formal training provided by FINDER staff.	User survey item 20
	Training Need*	Ord-inal	Response to survey item addressing need for more training.	User survey item 46
Agency/ Control		Nom-inal	Name of user's employing police agency.	User survey
	Agency Type*	Nom-inal	Police or Sheriff	User survey item 8
	Agency Sworn*	Scale	Number of sworn personnel in user's employing agency.	User survey item 9 & FDLE
	Agency Advocate*	Ord-inal	Response to survey item (exploratory)	User survey item 38
Time as LEO/ Control		Scale	Number of years user has been employed as sworn law enforcement officer	User survey
	Law Enforce-ment Experience	Scale	Number of years of law enforcement experience.	User survey item 15
Time as user/ Control		Scale	Period of time elapsed between first log-in as FINDER user (measured in days, weeks or months)	FINDER query logs & User survey
	User Months	Scale	Constrained to number of months measured from user's first login after December 1, 2004 and measured to February 28, 2006 (max 15 months)	FINDER Query Logs

Table 8-13: Final Study Variables (continued)

123

Table 8-13: Final Study Variables (continued)

Initial Variable (Name/Type)	Final Measures	Level	Description	Source
Number of Agencies Sharing Info		Scale	Number of police agencies sharing information via FINDER	PSTC & FINDER Query Logs
	None		Number of agencies sharing information was incorporated into measures of query volume.	
Technology/ Control		Nom-inal	Other information sharing technology available to user (i.e., other system name). Alternatively, weighted value of technologies	User survey

CHAPTER 9

Predicting Success

This chapter describes and discusses the statistical analyses that were used in an effort to answer the research question: What factors influence User-Level Success in the FINDER system? The answers are suggested by testing the hypothesized relationships between the variables and their respective measures that have been discussed in earlier pages. A brief recap may be helpful to summarize the changes in hypotheses and variables that became necessary in the evolution of the study from its conceptual design to final analyses.

The key changes are in the definition and measurement of the critical variables of interest: User-Level Success and System Use. The beginning study design envisioned these as being two distinct variables, represented by single measures. However, analyses of the actual, available success and System Use data demonstrated that both success and System Use might have more than one valid measure. Consequently, two new measures for User-Level Success, the Success Index and the Performance/Efficiency Index, were identified. In addition, three objective measures for System Use evolved from the Query Logs: Total Queries, Query Volume, and Active Months. While these objective data were available for only 252 of the 402 survey respondents, an additional measure of System Use (Frequency of Use) was available for all survey respondents.

Since the initial hypotheses were based on User-Level Success and System Use as single measures, they required expansion to test for predicted relationships across the combinations of new User-Level Success and System Use measures. Testing across the combinations of measures could help identify "best" measures of the constructs and be used to build related metrics. In addition, if the several outcome measures were individually reliable and valid, hypothesis testing across the combinations of measures was expected to produce consistent results in terms of the explanatory variables; i.e., those which predict FINDER success.

Thus, the initial set of nine hypotheses became twenty-six to permit statistical testing of all the combinations of "new" variables described above. These tests used multivariate regression ("regression") techniques. Four regression models were constructed to test predictions on the two User-Level Success measures using the two sets of System Use measures (the Query Log set and the data from the survey). Three additional models were required to test predictions on the three final System Use measures that survived the model-building process.[1] In addition, a structural equation model ("SEM") was used to explore the nonrecursive relationship between System Use and User-Level Success proposed by Goodhue's (1995) Task-technology Fit Model.

THE FINAL HYPOTHESES

The initial hypotheses H_1 through H_5 predicted relationships of the independent variables (including System Use) to User-Level Success. As noted above, each of these hypotheses was expanded to test for both measures of User-Level Success (Success Index and Performance/Efficiency Index) and, specifically in H_2, three System Use measures (Total Queries, Active Months, Frequency of Use) as predictors of success. Initial hypotheses H_6 through H_9 predicted a single measure of System Use as a mediating variable. Each of these hypotheses was also expanded to test for relationships of the independent variables to three System Use measures. Both the initial hypotheses and the expanded set are shown in Table 9-1. The expanded set has been stated in the null.

---

[1] Some variables were excluded from models because correlation analyses and model-building suggested they offered no explanatory power and did not contribute to this discussion. These variables were marked with an asterisk in Table 8-12.

Table 9-1: Initial & Final Hypotheses

Initial H_1	A FINDER user's task-fit measure will be positively and significantly related to the number of successes reported by that user.
Final H_{0_1A}	A user's FINDER Task-fit does not influence that user's Success Index.
Final H_{0_1B}	A user's FINDER Task-fit does not influence that user's Performance/Efficiency Index.
Initial H_2	A FINDER user's usage rate will be positively and significantly related to the number of successes reported by that user.
Final H_{0_2A}	A user's Total Queries does not influence that user's Success Index.
Final H_{0_2B}	A user's Active Months does not influence that user's Success Index.
Final H_{0_2C}	A user's Frequency of Use does not influence that user's Success Index.
Final H_{0_2D}	A user's Total Queries does not influence that user's Performance/Efficiency Index.
Final H_{0_2E}	A user's Active Months does not influence that user's Performance/Efficiency Index.
Final H_{0_2F}	A user's Frequency of Use does not influence that user's Performance/Efficiency Index.
Initial H_3	A FINDER user's computer expertise measure will be positively and significantly related to the number of successes reported by that user.
Final H_{03A}	A user's Computer Expertise does not influence that user's Success Index.
Final H_{03B}	A user's Computer Expertise does not influence that user's Performance/Efficiency Index.
Initial H_4	A FINDER user's receipt of FINDER training will be positively and significantly related to the number of successes reported by that user.
Final H_{04A}	A user's receipt of FINDER training does not influence that user's Success Index.
Final H_{04B}	A user's receipt of FINDER training does not influence that Performance/Efficiency Index.

Table 9-1 (continued): Initial & Final Hypotheses

Initial H_5	A FINDER user's job assignment will be positively and significantly related to the number of successes reported by that user.
Final H_{05A}	A user's Job Assignment does not influence that user's Success Index.
Final H_{05B}	A user's Job Assignment does not influence that user's Performance/Efficiency Index.
Initial H_6	A user's FINDER task-fit measure will be positively and significantly related to that user's usage rate.
Final H_{06A}	A user's FINDER Task-fit does not influence that user's Total Queries.
Final $H_{06B:}$	A user's FINDER Task-fit does not influence that user's Active Months.
Final H_{06C}	A user's FINDER Task-fit does not influence that user's Frequency of Use.
Initial H_7	A user's receipt of FINDER training will be positively and significantly related to that user's usage rate.
Final H_{07A}	A user's receipt of FINDER Training does not influence that user's Total Queries.
Final H_{07B}	A user's receipt of FINDER Training does not influence that user's Active Months.
Final H_{07C}	A user's receipt of FINDER Training does not influence that user's Frequency of Use.
Initial H_8	A FINDER user's computer expertise measure will be positively and significantly related to that user's usage rate.
Final H_{08A}	A user's Computer Expertise does not influence that user's Total Queries.
Final H_{08B}	A user's Computer Expertise Training does not influence that user's Active Months.
Final H_{08C}	A user's Computer Expertise does not influence that user's Frequency of Use.

Table 9-1 (continued): Initial & Final Hypotheses

Initial H_9	A FINDER user's job assignment, a FINDER user's usage rate will be significantly related to that user's system use.
Final H_{09A}	A user's Job Function does not influence that user's Total Queries.
Final H_{09B}	A Job Function does not influence that user's Active Months.
Final $H_{09C:}$	A user's Job Function does not influence that user's Frequency of Use.

REGRESSION MODELS AND RESULTS

SPSS 13.5 was used for the regression analyses. SPSS provides "automatic" model building algorithms, but the algorithms were not used because they do not necessarily build conceptually sound models. In addition, the algorithms (such as the "stepwise" method) do not recognize dummy variables (dichotomously-coded, nominal variables) in their groupings (Norusis, 2005). Since the independent variables in this study incorporated several nominal measures (e.g., job assignment, required use) coded as group dummies, the regression models were manually constructed.

The addition of variables to a regression model increases R^2 values, even if those variables are not important to the model (Gliner & Morgan, 2000; Kachigan, 1986; Kline, 2005). Thus, the manual model-building included a test for statistical significance for the change in R^2 as variables were added. Variables that did not contribute a statistically significant amount of explanatory power to the model were excluded.

Where alternative measures for the same concept were available (e.g., training, agency, job assignment), the measure used in the models was that which contributed the most to explanatory power. In this fashion, combinations of variables were added and excluded from each model to find the best, explanatory "fit" of the variables to the success and System Use measures. This manual process approximates that used by the SPSS algorithms, but allows control over the conceptual validity of the models (Norusis, 2005).

Residual data and partial coefficient plots and statistics were examined after each of the seven models was refined. These examinations helped confirm the linear relationships of the study variables and the predictive validity of the models (e.g., Gliner & Morgan, 2000; Norusis, 2005; van Belle, 2002). The residual data are not discussed unless they were remarkable in some fashion.

Seven regression models were constructed to test hypotheses. The first four models predict User-Level Success. The final three models predict System Use. The study variables used in the models are discussed relative to their model results and hypotheses. Control variables and other relationships that were not hypothetically posed are also addressed.

Models 1 through 4 were constructed to test H_{01} through H_{05B}. The first model regresses the objective, Query Log-based measures on the

Success Index. The second model uses the survey-based Frequency of Use data to predict the Success Index. The third model regresses the objective, Query Log data on the Performance/Efficiency Index. The fourth model predicts the Performance/Efficiency Index using survey-based Frequency of Use data. The results for these four models are shown in Table 9-2.

Table 9-2: Results of Regression Testing for User-Level Success Measures

Independent Variables	Success Index		Performance/Efficiency Index	
	Model 1 (n=252)	Model 2 (N=402)	Model 3 (n=252)	Model 4 (N=402)
Total Queries	.132*	-	.064	-
Active Months	.290***	-	.180***	-
Frequency of Use	-	.441***	-	.295***
FINDER Task-fit	.367***	.232***	.677***	.606***
Computer Expertise	.002	.024	.032	.044
Investigative Assignment	.124*	.172***	.134**	.061
Avg. Monthly Workload	.089	.053	.062	.034
FINDER Training	-.139**	-.035	-.088*	-.048
Law Enforcement Experience	-.049	-.042	.024	-.024
User Months	.118*	-	.000	-
Required Use	-.078	-.077*	-.011	-.035
Technology Options	.035	.019	.042	.020
R^2	.489	.456	.701	.665

*$p<.05$ **$p<.01$ ***$p<.001$
Standardized Coefficient Values (Beta) Displayed

Table 9-3 reflects the acceptance or non-acceptance of the alternative hypotheses across the four regression models. First, these findings will be discussed regarding the User-Level Success and System Use measures. Second, the findings will be discussed in terms of each group of hypotheses.

Table 9-3: Summary of Hypothesis Testing for User-Level Success Measures

Hypotheses		Success Index		Performance/ Efficiency Index	
		Model 1	Model 2	Model 3	Model 4
		Null hypothesis rejected?			
$H_{a\text{-}1A}$ & $H_{a\,1B}$	FINDER Task Fit $\rightarrow$	Yes	Yes	Yes	Yes
$H_{a\,2A}$ & $H_{A\,2D}$	Total Queries $\rightarrow$	Yes	-	No	-
$H_{a\,2B}$ & $H_{a\,2E}$	Active Months $\rightarrow$	Yes	-	Yes	-
$H_{a\,2C}$ & $H_{a\,2F}$	Frequency of Use $\rightarrow$	-	Yes	-	Yes
$H_{a\,3A}$ & $H_{a\,3B}$	Computer Expertise $\rightarrow$	No	No	No	No
$H_{a\,4A}$ & $H_{a\,4B}$	FINDER Training $\rightarrow$	Yes*	No	Yes*	No
$H_{a\,5A}$ & $H_{a\,5B}$	Job Function $\rightarrow$	Yes	Yes	Yes	No

* Negative relationship

User-Level Success and System Use

Optimally, a single, reliable, and valid measure of User-Level Success could be developed for gauging the value of police information sharing to its users. The regression models suggest that while *both* the Success Index and Performance/Efficiency Index are good measures of User-Level Success, the models incorporating the Performance/Efficiency Index offer higher explanatory power. As noted earlier, the Success Index was considered a subset of the Performance/Efficiency Index. The regression models support the proposition that the Performance/Efficiency Index reflects both the successful outcomes captured by the Success Index *and* additional gains in User-Level Success through increased efficiency.

In terms of R^2 value, these two success measures are consistently predicted by both objective and survey-based System Use data. This suggests that the survey-based measure of System Use, Frequency of Use, is a valid surrogate for the objective, Query Log-based measures. This is an important finding. Given the time and resources that were necessary to collect the Query Log Data, the survey-based estimation of system was a much more efficient way to represent System Use in its relationship to user-level performance (at least in the context of FINDER's distributed architecture). The System Use measures are discussed at greater length below.

- H_{0_1A}: *A user's FINDER Task-fit does not influence that user's Success Index.* The null is rejected; FINDER Task-fit was found to be a positive, statistically significant predictor of the Success Index across all four models.
- H_{0_1B}: *A user's FINDER Task-fit does not influence that user's Performance/Efficiency Index.* The null is rejected; FINDER Task-fit was found to be a positive, statistically significant predictor of the Performance/Efficiency Index across all four models.

Three of the four regression models found the task-fit measure to be the most important predictor of User-Level Success. These findings were expected; the relationship of task-fit to individual performance is the foundation of the Task-technology Fit model (Goodhue, 1995) used to frame this study. In practical terms, the importance of task-fit means that users who reported high levels of the *usefulness* and *usability* of FINDER were also likely to report high levels of success. Usefulness items in the survey assessed the value of FINDER data to the user's task-set. Usability items addressed ease of use and functionality.

- H_{0_2A}: A user's Total Queries does not influence that user's Success Index. The null is rejected; Total Queries was found to be a positive, statistically significant predictor of the Success Index.

- H_{0_2B}: A user's Active Months does not influence that user's Success Index. The null is rejected; Active Months was found to be a positive, statistically significant predictor of the Success Index.

- H_{0_2C}: A user's Frequency of Use does not influence that user's Success Index. The null is rejected; Frequency of Use was found to be a positive, statistically significant predictor of the Success Index.

- H_{0_2D}: A user's Total Queries does not influence that user's Performance/Efficiency Index. The null is not rejected; the relationship of Total Queries to the Performance/Efficiency Index was not statistically significant ($p < .173$).

- H_{0_2E}: A user's Active Months does not influence that user's Performance/Efficiency Index. The null is rejected; Active Months was found to be a positive, statistically significant predictor of the Performance/Efficiency Index.

- H_{0_2F}: A user's Frequency of Use does not influence that user's Performance/Efficiency Index. The null is rejected; Frequency of Use was found to be a positive, statistically significant predictor of the Performance/Efficiency Index.

Hypotheses H_{0_2A} through H_{0_2F} collectively predict the influence of different System Use variables on the two User-Level Success measures. With one exception (H_{0_2D}), both the objective and survey-based measures of System Use were significant predictors of User-Level Success. This exception is discussed first.

The non-significant result for Total Queries in Model 3 can be approached by comparing it to the statistically significant result for Total Queries in Model 1. Only one variable differs between the models: User-Level Success. Model 1 uses the Success Index (success-as-performance outcomes) and Model 3 uses the Performance/Efficiency Index (success as performance outcomes *and* efficiency). The apparent difference between the measures is the inclusion of an unspecified efficiency dimension in the latter. It is the presence of "efficiency" in the success variable that offers an explanation for the statistical non-significance of Total Queries in Model 3.

Conceptually, increasing the level of queries to achieve success becomes inefficient at some point. It is unlikely that a linear relationship between queries and success extends across the possible range of either. The data used for the Performance/Efficiency Index were constrained to a value of 7.0 by their item scales. The Total Query measure was not constrained. Non-linearity and a diminishing return on Total Queries were assured at some point in their relationship.

Although the effect of dissimilar ranges in the variable measurements was shared by the models, Model 1 did not measure efficiency; it measured only whether certain outcomes had occurred, and it did not capture frequency of those outcomes. In other words, given an X value of Total Queries in Model 1, the Success Index would be the same for X Total Queries whether the user had made 1 arrest or 100 arrests. Clearly, 100 arrests for X Queries are more efficient than 1 arrest, but Model 1 does not measure efficiency, and Total Queries is shown as a statistically significant influence on success regardless of implicit efficiency or inefficiency.

Model 2, however, *did* measure efficiency. The statistical insignificance of Total Queries in that model affirms that, all other things held constant, an increase in Total Queries does not contribute to efficiency. Further, during the iterative model-building process described above, it was noted that when the Workload control was excluded from Model 4, Total Queries became statistically significant ($p < .045$). This suggested that the Workload control offers an anchor (reference) point from which an "efficient" volume of queries can be estimated relative to the user's workload.

Alternatively, the model could be flawed, or the relationship of Total Queries to success could be spurious. However, the evidence indicates that a *volume*-based measure of System Use– such as Total Queries – can be used to estimate both outcomes and efficiency *if* the proper controls and scaling are in place.

The measures of Frequency of Use (Active Months and Frequency of Use) were statistically significant in all four models. Further, as noted above, it appeared the Frequency of Use survey measure was as good a predictor of success as were the combined data (Active Months and Total Queries) from the Query Logs. During the model-building process, it was observed in Models 1 and 3 that the exclusion of Total Queries resulted in significantly reduced effect in the Active Months variable. This produced a question about why Frequency of Use in Models 2 and 4, alone, offered as much predictive power as Active Months and Total Queries combined. In pragmatic terms, why would a five-point, rough interval scale from the survey emerge as a viable predictor with as much – or more – predictive power as the laboriously constructed, objective Query Log measures?

An explanation is offered. The Active Months variable measures Frequency of Use by months. The Frequency of Use variable from the survey, while limited to five intervals, is a finer measure by which the user estimates frequency on what is, effectively, a daily basis. Thus, Active Months is a specific measure of broad frequency periods (months), and Frequency of Use is a rough measure of narrow frequency periods (days). The findings of the four models suggest that measuring Frequency of Use within short periods of time may be the simplest way to estimate System Use.

- H_{03A}: A user's Computer Expertise does not influence that user's Success Index. The null is not rejected; the relationship of Computer Expertise to the Success Index was not statistically significant.
- H_{03B}: A user's Computer Expertise does not influence that user's Performance/Efficiency Index. The null is not rejected; the relationship of Computer Expertise to the Performance/Efficiency Index was not statistically significant.

The significance values for Computer Expertise ranged from $p<.454$ to $p<.628$ across all four models. The inclusion of this variable in the models was supported by the significance tests for changes in the R^2 values, but the inclusion or exclusion of Computer Expertise did not move any other variables into or out of significance. These findings indicate that a FINDER user's self-reported level of computer literacy has no significant power in predicting that user's success level.

One explanation for the statistical insignificance of the computer expertise measure is that FINDER was designed by its users to be user friendly and require little, if any, training. If this is true, then computer expertise would not play a significant role in successful FINDER use. Alternatively, the Computer Expertise measure may not be valid. This measure was generated through three self-report survey items, and there may be dimensions of computer literacy not captured by the small set of items.

It is possible that some baseline level of computer literacy is a necessary constant for contemporary law enforcement employees, regardless of their self-assessments of computer expertise. In this study, respondents were, at a minimum, capable of locating and responding to the online survey. The core computer skills necessary to complete the survey may have been, in and of themselves, also adequate for achieving success with FINDER. If so, increases in computer expertise beyond a core skill set would have had no significant effect in the statistical analyses.

- H_{04A}: A user's receipt of FINDER training does not influence that user's Success Index. Mixed results. The null cannot be rejected.
- H_{04B}: A user's receipt of FINDER training does not influence that Performance/Efficiency Index. Mixed results. The null cannot be rejected.

The results for the FINDER Training variable (whether training was provided by members of the FINDER staff) showed a mixed, negative relationship with the success variables. These results were not expected nor readily explained. The model findings reflect that when the Query Log data are used in the models (Models 1 and 3), FINDER Training is statistically significant in predicting a *reduction* in success. This negative relationship is also evident (though not significant) in the other two models. Substituting the Frequency of Use data for Query Log data in those models eliminated the statistical significance of FINDER Training but not the negative relationship. It appeared that the control for User Months (an indicator of FINDER experience) was the most important influence in moving FINDER Training in and out of statistical significance.

Conceptually, these data suggest that FINDER users become less successful after receiving the training, or that the users who attended FINDER training were different in some aspect that is not accounted for in the data and that is not directly related to their receipt of the training. For example, those users who attended the training may have sought training in an (unsuccessful) effort to improve weak investigative skills. Conversely, those users who did not seek training may have possessed a core set of skills or abilities that enhanced their success. It was also possible that the training curriculum was counterproductive to successful FINDER use.

Four steps were taken in an effort to explain these findings. First, the data were exhaustively re-examined to ensure that no coding errors had taken place. Second, the survey responses were reviewed to look for any patterns among those fifty-two survey respondents who had received FINDER training, particularly with regard to characteristics that were not included in the models. Third, the correlations and partial regression plots between the Training variables and other variables were reviewed for evidence of the negative relationships. None of these steps produced information to explain either the negative relationships or differences in significance between the models.

The fourth step was interviews with the FINDER staff's trainer and an agency-level FINDER administrator who had conducted training at his agency. Both advised that training sessions were provided both to inform personnel about FINDER's existence and to teach them how it is used. The FINDER trainer noted that "fifty or sixty" new users could be "signed up" at a training session. The agency trainer reported that he had "signed up" seventy new users through his training sessions. The FINDER trainer advised that "some" experienced users had attended his sessions, but new users were the target.

The agency-level trainer expressed frustration that few of his new users were actually using the system. He reported ninety-one registered users in his agency, but Query Logs only reflected activity by eleven users (four surveys were returned from his agency in which the registered users claimed they were not familiar with FINDER).

The FINDER trainer was perplexed when asked specifically about the negative relationship between System Use, success, and FINDER training. He suggested that one explanation is "the training guy [himself] needs to be fired." Otherwise, he could not offer a viable explanation and reiterated that FINDER agencies were asking for repeat training engagements because of the system's popularity and user successes.

- H_{05A}: A user's Job Assignment does not influence that user's Success Index. The null is rejected; the Investigative job title classification was found to be a positive, statistically significant predictor of the Success Index in three of the four models.
- H_{05B}: A user's Job Assignment does not influence that user's Performance/Efficiency Index. The null is rejected; the Investigative job title classification was

found to be a positive, statistically significant predictor of the Performance/Efficiency Index in three of the four models.

The Investigative Function dummy variable that tested as statistically significant in three of the four models was the job function (item 12) category selected by survey respondents. This variable provided the most explanatory power in the models. Although Model 4 did not find Investigative Function as statistically significant, significance was approached (p<.067).

All combinations of the various job assignment variables were tested in the models. The seven job *classifications* (patrol, property investigations, persons investigations, etc.) identified Property Investigations as significant in two of the models, but more explanatory power was achieved through the broader Investigative Function measure. Also noted was the consistent, negative relationship between the Patrol Function and the success measures. Although Patrol Function did not achieve statistical significance and did not contribute to the power of the models, it was clear that respondents in patrol assignments were reporting lower levels of success than their counterparts in investigative, analytical, and administrative positions.

The general finding that users in investigative job assignments experienced higher levels of success was expected. FINDER was created by and for investigators. Its origins as a pawn data sharing application were evident in the large proportion of survey respondents who were assigned to property crime investigations. The negative relationship of patrol assignments to success (though not statistically significant) was also expected. FINDER has not been widely deployed for wireless applications (i.e., in patrol cars) and, as Zaworski (2004) found, patrol officers are disinclined to routinely leave their patrol duties to use a desktop computer.

Neither the data nor other evidence gathered during this study provided clues as to why the Investigative Function was not statistically significant in the fourth model, or why the level of significance differed between the models. It was noted that as the negative influence of FINDER Training decreased, the positive influence of the Investigative Function increased. Given the poorly understood role of FINDER Training relative to success, the inverse relationship between FINDER Training and the Investigative Function could be spurious.

System Use

Three regression models were constructed to test the System Use hypotheses H_{06} through H_{09C}. The first model predicts Total Queries; the second model predicts Active Months; and the third model predicts Frequency of Use. The results for these three models are shown in Table 9-4.

Table 9-4: Results of Regression Testing for System Use Measures

Independent Variables	Total Queries Model 5 (n=252)	Active Months Model 6 (N=252)	Frequency of Use Model 7 (n=402)
FINDER Task-fit	.166**	.281***	.428***
FINDER Training	.067	.001	-.015
Computer Expertise	-.081	-.153*	-.098*
Investigative Assignment	.134*	.282***	.311***
Avg. Monthly Workload	.075	.115	.086*
Law Enforcement Experience	-.116	-.198**	-.042
User Months	.338***	-.013	-
Required Use	.037	.059	.051
Technology Options	-.002	-.092	-.029
R^2	.183	.206	.320

*p<.05 **p<.01 ***p<.001
Standardized Coefficient Values (Beta) Displayed

The relatively low R^2 values for the System Use models and their rank order was expected. The statistical significance of User Months to Total Queries was expected and is not particularly informative. With other user characteristics held constant, the total query volume of users should increase the longer they use the system. The results for the variables of hypothetical interest and their relationships with the control variables are discussed below. Table 9-5 reflects the acceptance or non-acceptance of the alternative hypotheses across the three System Use regression models.

Table 9-5: Summary of Hypothesis Testing for System Use Measures

		Model 5 (n=252)	Model 6 (N=252)	Model 7 (n=402)
		Total Queries	Active Months	Freqncy of Use
Hypotheses		Null hypothesis rejected?		
$H_{a-6A, B, C}$	FINDER Task Fit $\rightarrow$	Yes	Yes	Yes
$H_{a\,7A, B, C}$	FINDER Training $\rightarrow$	No	No	No
$H_{a\,8A, B, C}$	Computer Expertise $\rightarrow$	Mixed	Yes*	Yes*
$H_{a\,9A, B, C}$	Job Function $\rightarrow$	Yes	Yes	Yes

* Negative relationship

- H_{06A}: A user's FINDER Task-fit does not influence that user's Total Queries. The null is rejected; FINDER Task-fit was found to be a positive, statistically significant predictor of Total Queries.
- H_{06B}: A user's FINDER Task-fit does not influence that user's Active Months. The null is rejected; FINDER Task-fit was found to be a positive, statistically significant predictor of Active Months.
- $H_{06C:}$ A user's FINDER Task-fit does not influence that user's Frequency of Use. The null is rejected; FINDER

Task-fit was found to be a positive, statistically significant predictor of Frequency of Use.

The acceptance of the three alternative hypotheses for the relationship of FINDER Task-fit to the System Use measures was expected and unremarkable. Task-fit measures usefulness and usability; System Use was expected to be a positive function of both of these task-fit dimensions.

- H_{07A}: A user's receipt of FINDER Training does not influence that user's Total Queries. The null is not rejected; the relationship of FINDER Training to Total Queries was not statistically significant.
- H_{07B}: A user's receipt of FINDER Training does not influence that user's Active Months. The null is not rejected; the relationship of Finder Training to Active Months was not statistically significant.
- H_{07C}: A user's receipt of FINDER Training does not influence that user's Frequency of Use. The null is not rejected; the relationship of FINDER Training to Frequency of Use was not statistically significant.

Although the System Use regression models did not report training to be statistically significant, it was noted that the (very small) coefficients for FINDER Training were positive in their relationships to the objective System Use measures of Models 5 and 6 (Total Queries and Active Months) but negative for the survey-based measure of System Use (Frequency of Use). The mixed and weak influence of training in these three models suggests that the negative influence of training on User-Level Success (Models 1-4) is not directly related to an interaction between training and System Use. In other words, the regression models indicate a direct effect of training on User-Level Success, but the training effect is not significantly mediated by System Use.

- H_{08A}: A user's Computer Expertise does not influence that user's Total Queries. The null is not rejected; the relationship of Computer Expertise to Total Queries was not statistically significant.

- H_{08B}: A user's Computer Expertise does not influence that user's Active Months. The null is rejected; Computer Expertise was found to be a negative, statistically significant predictor of Active Months.
- H_{08C}: A user's Computer Expertise does not influence that user's Frequency of Use. The null is rejected; Computer Expertise was found to be a negative, statistically significant predictor of Frequency of Use.

The possibility of a negative relationship between computer expertise and System Use was noted in the development of the study variables. Researchers have proposed or found (Goodhue, 1995; Venkatesh & Davis, 2000) that more sophisticated or experienced System Users may use their technology systems *less* than unsophisticated users. Reduced System Use by expert users was posited as the result of either more efficient use or an expression of system dissatisfaction by more demanding, sophisticated users.

From this perspective, the findings were expected that Computer Expertise significantly and negatively influenced System Use in the Active Months and Frequency measures (Models 6 and 7). This relationship supports expert users as being more efficient in their FINDER use than less expert users; at least in terms of the frequency reflected by the measures in Models 6 and 7. Alternatively, the negative relationship might reflect FINDER dissatisfaction (and reduced use) among the more sophisticated users. However, if this were the case, Computer Expertise should have been negatively related to the FINDER Task-fit measure and the success measures in Models 1 through 4. It is possible that the relationship between Computer Expertise and System Use was spurious in these models, and it is recalled that the Computer Expertise index may have measured more dimensions than computer literacy.

Of interest was why Computer Expertise was not significant in only one of the three models, the Model 5 prediction of Total Queries ($p<.185$). This issue was considered in terms of the System Use measures: Models 6 and 7 predicted System Use as frequency (Frequency of Use and Active Months) while Model 5 predicted System Use as *volume* (Total Queries).

A review of partial correlation plots for the models suggested an explanation. The Frequency of Use variables were constrained (0.0 to 1.0 for Active Months and 1 to 5 for Frequency of Use) while Total

Queries data were not. Outlier cases were visible in the Total Queries plot and were posited as "cancelling" the controlling effect of Computer Expertise on use. In other words, the outlier data for Total Queries could statistically overpower the controlling effect of Computer Expertise on "normal" (non-outlier) users' query volume (Gujarati, 2003; Norusis, 2005). These outlier cases were discussed in the Query Log analysis.

To test this proposition, eight cases of outlier data were removed, and the remaining data were tested in a revision (Model 5a) to Model 5. With outliers excluded, both Computer Expertise and Law Enforcement Experience became statistically significant, and the R^2 improved to .233. These changes brought Model 5 into consistency with Models 6 and 7 across all measures. The change is shown in Table 9-6 where Model 5 (with outliers) is compared to Model 5a (without outliers).

Table 9-6: Revised Model 5: Excluding Outliers in Prediction of Total Queries

Independent Variables	Model 5 (N=252) Total Queries With Outliers	Model 5a (n=244) Total Queries With Outliers Removed
FINDER Task-fit	.166**	.234***
FINDER Training	.067	.007
Computer Expertise	-.081	-.121*
Investigative Assignment	.134*	.179*
Avg. Monthly Workload	.075	.101
Law Enforcement Experience	-.116	-.152*
User Months	.338***	.351***
Required Use	-.037	.017
Alternative Technology	-.002	-.054
R^2	.183	.233

*p<.05 **p<.01 ***p<.001
Standardized Coefficient Values (Beta) Displayed

The statistical effect of excluding Total Query outliers is conceptually important. Model 5a – like Models 6 and 7 – affirms that higher levels of computer expertise can reduce levels of System Use. However, Model 5a also suggests an important exception to the controlling effect of Computer Expertise. This exception was linked to interview information obtained through Success Tagging interviews.

Six of the outlier users that were removed from Model 5a were identified as detectives or analysts assigned to pawnshop investigations. Interviews with these users had revealed mechanical, or non-targeted, System Use that produced high query volumes. Relying on an earlier analogy, these users cast a large net – repeatedly and indiscriminately – without a specific target in mind, and were successful.

This type of high-volume user is not concerned with efficiency and confounds the presumed efficiency-gain effect of computer literacy. Consequently, this type of query behavior could confound other analyses that rely on System Use measures to predict or serve as proxy for User-Level Success. In this study, there was not a control for "pawn shop investigator."[2] The job assignment variables used in the models did not discriminate between this group (and perhaps other unidentified groups of high-volume users) and other users.

- H_{09A}: A user's Job Function does not influence that user's Total Queries. The null is rejected; Investigative Function was found to be a positive, statistically significant predictor of Total Queries.
- H_{09B}: A Job Function does not influence that user's Active Months. The null is rejected; Investigative Function was found to be a positive, statistically significant predictor of Active Months.
- H_{09C}: A user's Job Function does not influence that user's Frequency of Use. The null is rejected; Investigative Function was found to be a positive, statistically significant predictor of Frequency of Use.

Based on the results of Models 1 through 4 that reflected Investigative Function as a significant predictor of success, the results for

---

[2] Background investigators also reported mechanical query behavior, but they were not identified in the outlier cases.

Hypotheses H_{09A}, H_{09B}, and H_{09C} were expected in Models 5 through 7 and were unremarkable.

Control Variables

There were five control variables incorporated in the seven regression models: Technology Options, Workload, Required Use, Law Enforcement Experience, and User Months. As Tables 9-2 and 9-4 reflect, the control variables were, generally, not statistically significant in predicting User-Level Success or System Use, but they each added statistically significant explanatory power to the models. The first three control variables will be discussed separately; the two indicators of experience are considered together.

The Technology variable was not statistically significant in its relationship to either success or System Use measures. However, of interest was its relationship to System Use (negative) compared to User-Level Success (positive). The direction of these statistically insignificant relationships suggests that users who have more alternatives to FINDER use FINDER less, but also have (relatively speaking) more success with FINDER.

Conceptually, and recognizing that the technology variable was not significant in the models, a negative relationship between Technology Options and FINDER System Use is expected. The unexpected relationship is the possibility that a user who has more technology options is *more* successful with FINDER than users with fewer options. A check of the relationship between alternative technologies and computer expertise was conducted to consider whether users who have more available technology are more successful because they have more computer experience. However, the correlation between Technology Options and Computer Expertise was very weak and insignificant ($r= -.019$, $p<.709$).

It also possible that a complementary or synergistic effect occurs when FINDER and other systems are used in combination. For instance, it is recalled that almost half of the Success Tagging users achieved success with data from within their own agencies. These data were technically available through their agency RMS as a technology option. The limited findings here suggest that the interaction of multiple technologies in police information systems is a ripe research topic.

The Workload measure was statistically insignificant in six of the seven models; it was statistically significant only in predicting Frequency of Use in Model 7. Workload was conceived as an exploratory variable to control for difference in System Use that might be attributed to differences in the user's workload. The Workload survey item was scaled in un-equivalent intervals and asked respondents for a workload estimate based on each respondent's workload type (calls for service, cases, projects). Its reliability and validity are questionable. However, the model-building process identified the Workload measure as a statistically important explanatory variable. Further, as noted earlier, the importance of the workload measure might be related to its providing a baseline by which efficiency is assessed or perceived.

The Required Use variable was also a statistically insignificant predictor in six of the seven models and was found significant only in its prediction of the Success Index in Model 2. This result was not expected. Any significance in the Required Use measure was expected in the System Use outcomes, not in predicting User-Level Success, and not without a parallel result for System Use.

Additional study of the Required Use survey responses found that twenty-two (48%) of those users reporting that they were required to use FINDER were from only three agencies. The five supervisors of those twenty-two "required use" respondents were known due to their involvement and responses to other components of this study. Each of these supervisors was asked, within a series of general questions about FINDER, whether they or their agencies required its use. Four of the five supervisors advised that no one in their agency or command were required to use the system. The fifth supervisor advised that background investigators (representing two of the twenty-two "required use" users) *were* required to incorporate a FINDER search into background checks on law enforcement applicants. Of the five supervisors, three were direct supervisors of the users in question; two were indirect supervisors in the users' chains of command.

This issue was explored further to consider whether workplace norms might have influenced users to (apparently) incorrectly report they were required to use FINDER. Those who reported required use were compared against those who did not report required use for their response to survey item 38: "I work with someone who is always encouraging me to use FINDER." Cramer's V test was used to conduct this comparison and found a statistically significant difference between the groups on their responses (Cramer's V = .261, p<.01). A crosstab evaluation of the data reflected that responses to item 38 in the agreement range were much higher for the required use respondents; 45% of those who reported required use also agreed with item 38, compared to 26% of the users who reported voluntary use.

These findings suggested that the validity of the Required Use variable was questionable. However, it can be argued that if users *believe* they are required to use the system, then perhaps that is more important than whether they are actually required to use it. Thus, the required use variable remained as a control for System Use in the regression models, but its significance in Model 2 was not considered important. Perhaps more importantly, while Goodhue (1995) proposed an unspecified relationship between voluntariness and System Use, the definition of voluntary use did not consider *perceived* voluntariness (or perceived requirement) as found in this study. Future studies could be improved by considering workplace norms in the development of voluntary-use/required-use variables.

Law Enforcement Experience and Time as FINDER User were conceived as controls for User-Level Success that might be attributed to experience-based proficiencies rather than FINDER use. Law enforcement experience was measured as the user's number of years of law enforcement experience, and the user's time as a FINDER user was measured as User Months. The User Months data were available only for the 252 respondents who were matched with Query Log activity.

These experience measures are considered jointly because of their divergent results throughout the seven models. Law enforcement experience was found to be a statistically significant negative predictor of System Use in Models 6 and 7; an insignificant negatively-signed control in Models 1, 2, and 4; an insignificant, positively-signed influence in Model 3. User Months, which was included only in Models 1, 2, 5, and 6, also had divergent results.

User Months was significant in predicting the Success Index but insignificant (with a Beta of .000; p<.993) in its relationship with the Performance/Efficiency Index. User Months was highly significant in positively predicting Total Queries but negatively-signed and insignificant in predicting Active Months.

In effect, the only consistent finding about FINDER users' experience was that System Use, generally, was negatively related to law enforcement experience. The data provided no clues as to whether this relationship might be due to experienced users' sophistication and efficiency, or those senior users' discomfort or dissatisfaction with technology in general.

An examination of the experience variables revealed they were significantly correlated to agency size (number sworn) and Sheriff's Offices, with a significant and negative correlation to Police Departments. In other words, the most experienced respondents in terms of law enforcement *and* FINDER experience tended to be members of the larger Sheriff's Offices.

FINDER originated largely through efforts to share pawn data led by personnel in five of the state's larger Sheriff's Offices. Users from those five agencies comprised forty-one of the fifty-two (72%) survey respondents with at least fifteen User Months. Eighteen of these users were interviewed during the course of this study.

These interviews, conducted as needed between January and August 2006, addressed the several Query Log and Success Tag questions discussed earlier in this chapter. A common theme expressed by these senior FINDER users was their *commitment to information sharing*. These users repeatedly expressed their enthusiasm for the information exchange and that it was long overdue as a tool for Florida law enforcement. Several of them expressed hope that this study would help "prove" the value of information sharing to their Sheriffs.

Conversely, the newer FINDER users who were contacted during the course of the study were not aware of FINDER's origins or development. Many were unaware of UCF's role and required an explanation of that role before providing interview information.[3] These users perceived FINDER as a useful tool (like NCIC) but did not express a commitment to information sharing or an understanding of FINDER's development through a Consortium effort.

The proposition that "experience," at least in the context of FINDER's unique origin, might reflect a dimension of commitment to information sharing is not without support. The concept of information sharing champions being necessary for success has been discussed elsewhere in terms of agency-level participation (e.g., BJA, 2002). An unmeasured dimension, commitment to information sharing, may be associated with the most senior FINDER users. If so, then that

---

[3] It was discovered during the survey and follow-up interview process that "FINDER" had to be explicitly associated with other system labels such as "Pawn System," or "UCF System," or "Data Sharing Consortium."

unmeasured dimension may explain the divergent results for Law
Enforcement Experience and User Months that are found in the
regression models.

EXPLORING THE RELATIONSHIP BETWEEN SUCCESS
AND SYSTEM USE

The Task-technology Fit framework (Goodhue, 1995) used in this
study conceptualized – but did not explain – the relationship between
User-Level Success and System Use.   The logical relationship
describes System Use being required to generate success, but success is
likely to generate additional System Use. A better understanding of
this relationship is important because System Use frequently serves as a
surrogate measure for information system success.   The surrogate
measure is accepted under the assumption that increases in System Use
reflect increases in success.   The important, unanswered question is
how much additional success (if any) is being reflected by increases in
System Use. If the answer to that question is better understood, System
Use may be valuable as a reliable success metric.
    A nonrecursive structural equation path model (SEM) was used to
explore the relationship between User-Level Success and System Use.
Nonrecursive models estimate simultaneous relationships between
endogenous (dependent) variables and their shared exogenous
(independent) predictor variables.   In this study, User-Level Success
and System Use were the endogenous variables proposed by the task-fit
framework to have a feedback relationship.
    Table 9-7 considers the relationship between User-Level Success
and System Use by reporting R^2 values from regressions (Models 4 and
7) modified to include or exclude success or System Use appropriately.
The R^2 values indicate that User-Level Success is less dependent on
System Use (R^2 decreasing 8.9% when System Use is dropped) than
System Use is dependent on User-Level Success (R^2 decreasing 24.2%
when User-Level Success is dropped).

Table 9-7: Changes in R^2 Values in User-Level Success and System
Use Relationships

Inclusion/Exclusion of Exogenous Variable		Endogenous Variable	R^2
System Use <u>included</u> as exogenous variable	→	User-Level Success as endogenous variable	.665
System Use <u>excluded</u> as exogenous variable			.606
User-Level Success <u>included</u> as exogenous variable	→	System Use as endogenous variable	.422
User-Level Success <u>excluded</u> as exogenous variable			.320

Conceptually – not statistically and with scaling differences in mind – these R^2 data suggest that an additional increment of "success" produces more increments of "System Use" than System Use produces of success. Thus, conceptually, there is a relationship of diminishing returns. If a single success produces 100 more queries, those 100 queries will not reciprocally produce another success; perhaps 300 more queries will be required to accomplish that, with all other things (such as caseload, computer expertise, job assignment, etc.) held constant.

The potential of a diminishing-returns (or increasing-returns) relationship poses a challenge to employing System Use as a surrogate measure for success. For example, if it is found at a given time that a given number of successes are reported based on a given level of System Use, it cannot be assumed that a twofold increase in System Use reflects a twofold increase in successes. Some grasp of the *relative* relationship between the two measures is necessary.

Conceptual Model

A nonrecursive SEM path diagram was constructed to explore this relationship. The conceptual model shown in Figure 9-1 mirrors Goodhue's (1995) task-fit framework. Nonrecursive models present a variety of challenges in their design and interpretation, and it is difficult to satisfy their assumptions. Some of the key assumptions, and implications of their violation, are discussed here.

This study was initially proposed to consider the longitudinal relationship between User-Level Success and System Use, but a cross-sectional analysis was mandated because the Success Tag-based data was not reliable. Logically, the validity of a nonrecursive model is questionable when cross sectional data are used. The nonrecursive model is based on a feedback relationship that, by definition, measures change over time versus the cross sectional snapshot. Maruyama notes that the difficulty in satisfying assumptions may cause researchers to wonder "whether there really are nonrecursive models" (p. 101) that can be validly constructed with cross sectional data. Thus, absent longitudinal data, results from a nonrecursive model should be cautiously considered (Kline, 2005; Maruyama, 1998).

The nonrecursive model also assumes that equilibrium has been achieved in the relationship between the endogenous variables. The equilibrium assumption means that the relationship is stable, that there are no influences that cause the relative relationship between the endogenous variables to change. Equilibrium is difficult to argue in applied study; any number of influences can affect a claimed state of equilibrium. However, a stability index, produced by SEM software, provides an indication of equilibrium that can be considered with the model's results (Kline, 2005; Maruyama, 1998). [4]

---

[4] Kline (2005) reports studies indicating that the stability index does not adequately reflect equilibrium-based bias, but use of the stability index as a guide is not dismissed.

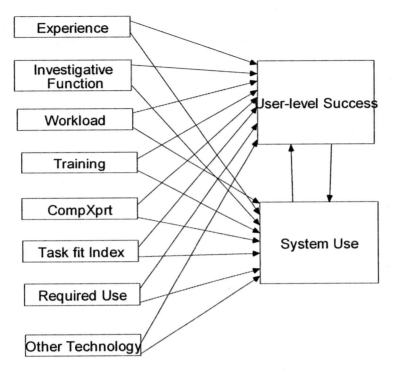

Figure 9-1: Conceptual Nonrecursive Task-fit Model

It is difficult to identify a nonrecursive model. Identification means that there are enough degrees of freedom in the model to estimate the unknown parameters. By their nature, most nonrecursive models are unidentified, and modifications are required to achieve identification.

Two, general methods can be used to achieve identification: constraining parameters or re-specifying the model with instrumental variables or otherwise removing relationships that require estimation. Kline notes that such procedures can "seem like a shell game: add this path, drop another, and – voila'! – the model is identified" (2005, p. 249). Thus, modifications should be true to a model that has been logically or theoretically supported.

The models shown Figure 9-1 (above) and Figure 9-2 (below) were not re-specified. All relationships proposed by Goodhue (1995) were retained in the final model. However, to obtain identification, the parameter for the relationship of success to System Use was set to a reference value of one, as generally suggested by Kline (2005). The constraint on the success parameter enhanced model fit and produced logical results that were consistent with underlying theory and regression findings.

The data used for the SEM analysis were those from Model 2 in the regressions. These data were used because of the available sample size (N=402) and the use of the Success Index rather than the Performance/Efficiency Index. Conceptually, the influence of the efficiency dimension in the Performance/Efficiency Index was expected to confound the nonrecursive relationship through an unspecified influence of efficiency on System Use.

Nonrecursive Model Results

The graphic results of the final model, with standardized coefficient values, are shown in Figure 9-2. The related statistics are provided in Table 9-8. The Stability Index and Goodness of Fit measures indicate that the final model was reasonably fit by the data.[5]

The results suggest the expected, statistically significant relationship between User-Level Success and System Use. The magnitude of the direct effect for Success $\rightarrow$ System Use is the largest; it estimates that a level of User-Level Success one standard deviation above the mean will produce an increase in System Use .267 standard deviations above its mean. The indirect effect on User-Level Success via System Use is estimated as .267 x .157 or .042. In other words, an increase in User-Level Success one standard deviation above its mean produces an indirect effect – through System Use – of an increase in User-Level Success .042 standard deviations above its mean (Kline, 2005).

---

[5] A Stability Index< 1.0; X^2 >.05; GFI>.900; AGFI>.900 and RMSEA<.05 indicate good model fit (Kline, 2005; Maruyama, 1998; Wan, 2002)

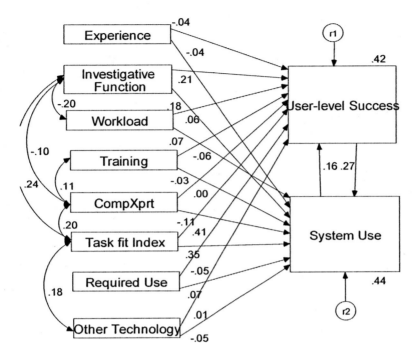

Figure 9-2: Final Nonrecursive SEM Results

These findings, subject to the several limitations and cautions expressed above, support the proposition that success achieved by FINDER users results in additional System Use, but the additional System Use does not produce commensurate increases in success, with all other influences held constant.

As noted above, the value of this finding is that it offers limited empirical evidence that employing System Use measures as surrogates for User-Level Success should acknowledge differences in the relative magnitudes of the feedback relationship. Given the data available through FINDER and its users, success predicts System Use better than System Use predicts success.

Table 9-8: Table of Statistics for Final Nonrecursive Model

Exogenous Variable	User-Level Success	System Use
User-Level Success	-	.267 ***†
System Use	.157**	-
FINDER Task-Fit	.405***	.350***
Investigative Function	.212***	.183***
Computer Expertise	.003	-.107**
Workload	.064	.065
Required Use	.053	-.067
FINDER Training	-.061	-.027
Law Enforcement Experience	-.042	-.035
Alternative Technology	.006	-.045
R^2	.423	.443
Stability Index =	.042	

Goodness of Fit Measures
$X^2 = 23.153$, $df = 22$, p>.393
GFI = .987
AGFI = .968
RMSEA =.012

**p<.01   ***p<.001   † Estimated significance

CHAPTER 10

Perpetuating Success

The initial pages of this book described the link between traffic tickets and terrorists – a link that that drives current U.S. policy to establish law enforcement information sharing systems in the all-crimes approach to improving public safety and advancing Homeland Security interests.

This study has looked at a combined set of data that depicts how law enforcement officers successfully achieve their all-crimes task objectives through the use of shared, low-level police information. The following pages summarize what the FINDER study has revealed about the value of sharing low-level police information, and offer recommendations intended to improve and perpetuate information sharing success.

USER-LEVEL SUCCESS

- *Sharing low-level police information produces successful policing outcomes.* Specific success reports submitted by 159 users included details about 384 arrests and 537 stolen property recoveries attributed to FINDER information. A survey of 402 users found that 68.4% had used FINDER information to make arrests, clear cases, develop investigative leads, discover a crime, or locate or identify a person of interest.

- *Sharing low-level police information produces gains in individual performance and efficiency.* Of the 402

FINDER users responding to the survey, 71.6% reported
that FINDER had helped improve their job performance.
Gains in efficiency attributed to FINDER were reported
by 82.6% of the users.

- *The importance of sharing information within one's own
  agency may be underestimated.* Specific success reports
  reflected that 48.2% of successes were based on
  FINDER's extraction of information from within the
  reporting user's own agency. User interviews indicated
  that FINDER acquired information from within the users'
  agency RMS that they could not otherwise access.

- *Sharing information with both local and distant agencies
  produces success.* Specific success reports reflected that
  37.3% of successes were based on information acquired
  from other local agencies. Distant agencies provided
  information leading to 14.5% of reported successes.

The combined data strongly support the value of sharing low-level
police information. These data affirmed that user-level success or
performance measures in police information sharing should encompass
a range of positive outcomes broader than arrests or case clearances.
FINDER's police users reported that investigative leads, property
recoveries, discovery of crime, and contact or background information
about both offending and non-offending subjects are important to
achieving performance and efficiency objectives.

This study also found contextual factors that can influence efforts
to measure the user-level value of information sharing. Prolific users
who served as their squad-level "FINDER person" were identified.
These users found information that produced arrests and case
clearances for *non-users*. In addition, users who had no assigned
caseload and who identified crimes and offenders by mining FINDER's
data were identified. These investigators adopted only those cases that
they had already "solved" and reported a 100% clearance rate. These
findings suggest that "objective" arrest and case clearance measures of
success must consider the user's context.

An unexpected finding was the prevalence of successes attributed
to FINDER's extraction of data from the users' own agencies. These
users reported that they were unable to access or efficiently gain access
to important data via their agency RMS. FINDER provided an efficient

method of getting this information. In addition, users in Police Departments reported that FINDER gave them access to critical data held by their local Sheriff's Office. They had previously been unable to acquire these data. These findings indicate that information sharing is important intra-agency and inter-agency, both locally and with distant information sources.

A key objective of this study was to determine what factors influence user-level success. If these factors can be identified, then strategies can be developed to optimize them and thereby increase success levels. The Task-Technology Fit (TTF) framework (Goodhue, 1995) was used to guide research aimed at identifying these factors. One of the two major TTF components was system use. Goodhue proposed that a technology user's system use predicts changes in that user's performance. However, this relationship was not specified and was acknowledged as complex and contextual. Conclusions related to the system use construct as applied to FINDER are reported below.

SYSTEM USE

- *Frequency of use was the best measure for "system use" in terms of predicting user-level success.* Data that reported each FINDER user's specific system activity over a fifteen-month period were analyzed during this study. These data represented 1.8 million specific queries for information by 1,352 users. Of the variety of system use measures that were extracted from or computed with these data and survey responses, the frequency of use measures were the best predictors of user-level success.

- *Users search for information from all available sources.* Most users, 76.8% in a secondary survey, reported that they usually search all FINDER agency data sources rather than selectively or incrementally search. Users were not dissuaded by the additional time required for broad searches.

- *Many users conduct repetitive searches to locate newly available information.* Repetitive searches constituted 23% of FINDER's system activity in a random sample of query logs. A secondary survey of users found that 34%

"usually" conduct repetitive searches for new information; an additional 43% reported that they conduct repetitive searches "depend[ing] on the case or situation."

- *System use behaviors vary with user job tasks.* Some users engaged in routine, high-volume, mechanical FINDER searches for any useful information. Others used FINDER to selectively search for specific information. While these methods produced divergent measures of system use, both also produced successes. The method chosen appeared dependent on the user's job assignment.

Information systems research consistently postulates that unspecified measures of "system use" predict users' satisfaction or successes with the system. This study had FINDER's objective system data (the Query Logs) from December 2004 to February 2006 to compare with user-level success. A number of objective measures were extracted or computed from the data and considered for their reliability and validity in reflecting the system use construct. User query volume – the number of inquiries each user made to each FINDER agency – was evaluated through several measures. These measures included users' average monthly query volume, total query volume over fifteen months, fifteen-month query volume indices, fifteen-month averages and moving averages, and query volume trends. None of these query *volume* measures were independently valid in predicting user-level success.

The objective Query Log data also provided a *frequency* of use measure. This was the percentage of months that each user made queries during that user's FINDER tenure. The frequency-by-month measure, when combined with the user's total query volume, was statistically significant in predicting success. In addition, survey respondents estimated their system use through a rough, days-of-use-per-week measure. That measure, which was independent of query volume, was the most powerful "system use" predictor of user-level success. A statistical control variable was used for the 11.4% of users who reported that they were *required* to use FINDER.

These findings suggest that the frequency of system logins may be the best system use metric when considering user-level performance. The volume of activity (query volume) following the login was not a good system use measure. The failure of volume measures to predict success might be due to differences in individual user's workloads, query methods, or job assignment. Those differences were revealed in system use behaviors that included repeated queries, mechanical queries, and targeted queries.

Of users responding to a secondary survey about query behaviors, 77% reported that they repeated queries in an effort to find newly available information about their topic of interest. An exploratory examination of their repeated query behavior indicated that repeated query behavior does not necessarily result in high query volume. Data were not available to estimate the effect of repeated queries on user-level success, but the prevalence of repeated query behavior suggests that it rewards users. This behavior also suggests that FINDER's functionality could be improved with the inclusion of monitoring or subscription routines that automatically check for new information on subjects of interest.

Mechanical, or indiscriminate, high-volume query behavior was also identified as affecting the measurement of system use. This type of behavior was primarily attributed to pawnshop and background investigators. Generally, they executed queries on every person, address, or piece of property listed in case files and waited to see if any information of interest was returned. Essentially, they engaged in high query volume, exploratory searches and were rewarded with high levels of success. This query behavior both allowed them to solve reported crimes and discover unreported crimes such as dealing in stolen property or violations of probation.

Conversely, other successful users reported that they used FINDER selectively when they had investigative leads that led them to target their searches for information. This type of user exhibited consistent frequency of use but a low volume of use. However, whether targeted or mechanical, most users (76.8%) reported that they executed searches against *all* available FINDER agencies. They did not typically query only a few agencies or start with local searches and expand the search incrementally.

These system use findings are important for three reasons. First, they identify a system use metric – frequency of use – that was valid in the FINDER analysis and can be considered for application elsewhere. The validity of this metric is supported by an understanding of user behaviors that can confound system use measures that are based on activity or volume. Second, an understanding of system use behaviors and the difference between frequency of use and volume of use can assist software developers with system design. System functionalities should include the capture of users' login activity and automated routines to eliminate the need for manually executed repeat queries. Third, system designers should recognize that users will probably seek *all* available information in their queries. Both system architecture and bandwidth requirements are likely to be affected by user demands.

The second major component of the TTF framework is task-technology fit. TTF proposes that information system users will have greater gains in performance when the system is usable (ease of use) and provides information that is useful in meeting the user's task needs. Task needs are affected by user characteristics including the user's work and technology experience, environment, and job functions. Conclusions about FINDER's task-technology fit and related user characteristics are provided below.

TASK-TECHNOLOGY FIT

- *Users who positively assessed FINDER's usefulness and ease of use experienced higher levels of success.* Empirical analyses consistently found that the user's assessment of system usefulness and usability was the most powerful predictor of user-level success. Usefulness addresses the value of the information provided by FINDER to meeting user task needs. Usability refers to the system's ease of use.

- *Users assigned to investigative functions were most likely to report user-level success.* FINDER users assigned to investigative functions achieved higher levels of success than those assigned to patrol, analytical, or administrative functions.

- *A FINDER user's level of computer expertise did not significantly influence the likelihood of achieving user-level success.* Users' computer expertise (computer literacy) was not a statistically significant influence in predicting user-level success. The computer expertise measurement was exploratory.

- *The user's type of agency and agency size did not influence the likelihood of achieving user-level success.*

Users from Police Departments, Sheriff's Offices, and state law enforcement agencies were included in this study. The sizes of these agencies ranged from six to 1,600 sworn officers. Neither the agency type nor the agency size statistically contributed to predictions of user-level success.

- *The influence of users' law enforcement experience, FINDER experience, and FINDER-related training on user-level success was not clarified with empirical tests.* Mixed results were produced in the empirical models that estimated the influence of experience and training on user-level success. Factors such as the commitment to information sharing by senior FINDER members who helped found the system and the selection of disengaged users for FINDER training were believed to have confounded the analyses.

Task-fit was consistently found to be a significant and highly influential predictor of user-level success. Task-fit measures included the users' job functions and assessments of FINDER's usefulness and usability in their task context. Controlling influences, such as the user's technology environment, agency type, and agency size did not have significant explanatory power in the empirical models.

Measures of the effect of law enforcement experience and length of FINDER experience were mixed in their prediction of both system use and user-level success. Interviews with users suggested that the "experience" measures in the FINDER context might have been confounded by an unmeasured user dimension characterized as "commitment to information sharing." A number of FINDER's most successful and senior users were involved in founding, designing, and implementing the system. The presence of a "commitment" dimension could have created spurious empirical relationships in the experience data.

The appearance of a *negative* relationship between users' who received FINDER training and their level of success was unexpected. The negative effect of training on success did not appear to be mediated through the frequency of system use, and none of the empirical data available suggested an explanation. One explanation of the relationship is that FINDER training is, of itself, somehow counterproductive. A second explanation – supported by limited, qualitative evidence – is that many users who received FINDER training were "signed up" as users at the same time they received the training. Some – perhaps many – of these new users did not demonstrate an interest in or need for FINDER. Consequently, their FINDER use and successes were limited. Specific data were not available to link newly-recruited users to FINDER training and their system use. The training topic remains unresolved.

A FINDER user's assignment to an investigative function was statistically significant in predicting that user's level of success. This finding was expected. FINDER was conceived by investigators and most of its users are investigators. FINDER has not been widely deployed in a wireless environment available to patrol officers. The data sets and software interface were designed and specified by investigators who founded the system. In this context, the task-fit of FINDER to investigators was assured, but the important finding is that good task fit *does* predict user-level success.

Further, usability (ease of use) and usefulness of data were *jointly* reported as dimensions that reflect of task-fit. Some researchers have suggested that ease of use is not particularly important to police users. However, based on the data gathered from FINDER users, ease of use appears to be an important dimension of task-fit and, consequently, ease of system use is important to user-level success.

PERPETUATING SUCCESS

The conclusions outlined above support the value of sharing low-level police information as evidenced by user-level success in the FINDER system. Several evidence-based recommendations are offered that can be used to enhance other information sharing efforts.

- *User-level success with police information sharing includes outcomes beyond traditional measures of arrests and case clearances.* System metrics should be designed to efficiently capture success events that include investigative leads, property recovery, locating or identifying people, the discovery or prevention of crimes, and efficiency gains.

- *Police information sharing successes can be increased by improving the task-technology fit.* Task-fit can be enhanced by relying on users to specify data needs, functionality, and the user interface. Ease of use appears to be important to end users.

- *The design of police information sharing systems should provide monitoring functionality to alert users to newly arriving information about subjects of interest.*

- *Police agency leaders and technology managers should recognize that sharing information within their own agencies could produce success.* As a first step to advancing information sharing objectives, agencies should examine their resident records management system to determine whether valuable, low-level information is readily available to their own agency members.

- *Police information sharing systems rely on the coordinated efforts of technology managers at each participating agency.* User-level success can be inhibited by the failure of these managers to ensure the availability of and access to timely and complete data. The governance structure of the information sharing project should clearly identify agency-level technology managers and routinely verify their continued support of the system. Quality assurance processes should be in place for both data accuracy and security control.

It is noted that findings emerged during the course of this study that could not be adequately explored or explained. These findings suggest topics for additional research that include:

- Data from user-reported Success Tags – while informative – was empirically unreliable. Additional research could identify better processes for reliably reporting success data.

- Improved efficiency was indicated to be an important dimension of user-level success. This study did not collect data to measure changes in efficiency attributed to police information sharing. Additional research could clarify the role of efficiency to improvements in user-level performance.

- Different user-level information-seeking techniques were identified in this study. They included mechanical queries, targeted queries, and repeated queries. Neither the value of these techniques toward achieving user-level success nor their effect on system-use measures could be established with the available data. Additional research may reveal if query techniques are embedded in system use data and whether specific techniques produce higher levels of success.

- Because reliable longitudinal data were not available in this study, the relationship of system use and other explanatory variables to user-level success was considered in a cross-sectional approach. Additional research using reliable data in a longitudinal design would help identify time-variant dimensions of the information sharing process.

- It is extremely important to note that this study examined how FINDER users acquired the data and the outcomes that resulted from the data acquisition but did not look at how the users analyzed or applied the data to achieve those outcomes. FINDER users, generally, discounted the need for automated "analytical tools." This is an area ripe for additional research. Analytical styles and methods employed to different ends by different users are a likely source of unexplained variance in the regression models.

The results and interpretation of the FINDER study are subject to limitations. Data and methodological limitations were discussed in context as they appeared in the research process, and other limitations include:

- This study focused on a single police information sharing system functioning in Florida's unique law enforcement and technology environments.
- The user survey was administered as a probability sample. However, data collected through the survey remains subject to unidentified non-response or response biases.
- The survey found that 88% of FINDER's users are voluntary users. These voluntary users may be more comfortable with technology than the general law enforcement population.

- At least 5% of the objective Query Log data were missing or inaccurate.
- Success Tag reports were highly subjective.
- Exploratory measures for computer expertise, technology options, and required use were employed in empirical analyses.

To keep findings, recommendations, and limitations in perspective, this study has looked at roughly 1,600 FINDER users, their 1.8 million system data records, 741 specific reports of FINDER "successes," survey responses from 402 active users, and interviews with more than 100 users who collectively represented nearly 120 Florida police agencies. What the study shows is that police information sharing works.

Law enforcement officers who have access to routine police data across multiple jurisdictions report improved performance and increased efficiency in their efforts to battle crime. By extension, and with the support of anecdotes provided by the American intelligence community, these gains in all-crimes police performance and efficiency should also be contributing to counterterrorism efforts. In sum, the research reported in this book offers sound evidence that that the U.S. law enforcement and intelligence communities are on the right track by working to expand information sharing capacity.

This study has also provided insight to the very nature of "success" in the police information sharing environment. Given acceptance that successful police information sharing is a good and important thing, the FINDER study identifies factors that may predict successful policing outcomes due to the use of shared information. The identification of those factors provides guidance to policy makers and IT administrators in building information systems that have a higher probability of producing benefit to their users. Those benefits translate to better protection of the American public from all crime.

APPENDICES

APPENDIX A: FINDER USER SURVEY RESULTS

	Have you:	Yes	Yes%	No	No%	Total Response	N.A./No answer	Applicable Responses
1.	Made an arrest?	148	45.7	176	54.3	396	78	324
2.	Solved a case?	172	51.8	160	48.2	402	70	332
3.	Recovered property?	140	43.9	179	56.1	402	83	319
4.	Identified a suspect?	217	63.6	124	36.4	402	61	341
5.	Located a person?	203	60.2	134	39.8	402	65	337
6.	Recovered a vehicle?	14	4.8	275	95.2	402	113	289
7.	Discovered a crime?	91	29.1	222	70.9	402	89	313

8. For what type of law enforcement agency do you work?

Police Department		Sheriff's Office		State Agency		Total Responses
Police	Police%	Sheriff	Sheriff%	State	State%	
120	29.9%	273	67.9%	9	2.2%	402

Items 9 & 10 reported agency name and username.				
11. Are you a sworn or non-sworn employee?				
Sworn		Non-sworn		
Sworn	Sworn%	Non-Sworn	Non-Sworn%	N
326	81.5%	74	18.5%	400

12. Which of the following best describes your job *function?*		
	Frequency	Percent
Patrol	61	15.2%
Investigations	242	60.2%
Administrative	40	10.0%
Analysis/Support	58	14.4%
Total	401	100.0%

13. What is your rank?		
	Frequency	Percent
Officer/Deputy/Agent	206	51.2%
Supervisor	12	3.0%
Corporal	30	7.5%
Sergeant	38	9.5%
Lieutenant	16	4.0%
Manager	1	0.2%
Captain	7	1.7%
Other Command	5	1.2%
Analyst	41	10.2%
Other	41	10.2%
No response	5	1.2%
Total	402	100.0%

Appendix A (continued)

14. What is your job title?

			Frequency	Percent
Patrol Function		Officer/Deputy	56	13.9%
		Traffic Officer	4	1.0%
		Marine Officer	2	0.5%
		Tactical Officer	1	0.2%
		School Officer/DARE	1	0.2%
Investigative Function	All Crimes		48	11.9%
	Property Crimes	Detective- All Property Crimes	101	25.1%
		Detective-Auto Theft	9	2.2%
		Detective-White Collar Crimes	11	2.7%
	Persons Crimes	Detective- All Persons Crimes	2	0.5%
		Detective-Violent Crimes	4	1.0%
		Detective-Homicide	12	3.0%
		Detective-Sex Crimes	2	0.5%
		Detective-Child Abuse	5	1.2%
		Detective-Robbery	7	1.7%
	Other Investigations	Detective-Computer Crimes	1	0.2%
		Detective-Narcotics/Vice	7	1.7%
		Agricultural Crimes	1	0.2%
		Intelligence Officer	13	3.2%
		Background Investigator	5	1.2%
		State Attorney Investigator	4	1.0%
		Crime Scene Investigator	2	0.5%
Analytic Function		Crime Analyst	35	8.7%
		Research Analyst	6	1.5%
		Investigative Assistant	2	0.5%
Admin/Other			59	14.7%
No Response			2	0.5%
Total			402	100.0%

15. What is your total number of years of law enforcement experience?		
Years of Experience	Frequency	Percent
<1 year	4	1.0%
1	2	0.5%
2	10	2.5%
3	12	3.0%
4	6	1.5%
5	16	4.0%
6	8	2.0%
7	15	3.7%
8	26	6.5%
9	19	4.7%
10	20	5.0%
11	19	4.7%
12	21	5.2%
13	12	3.0%
14	19	4.7%
15	15	3.7%
16	30	7.5%
17	25	6.2%
18	12	3.0%
19	11	2.7%
20+	97	24.1%
No response	3	0.7%
Total	402	100.0

17. Are you required by your agency or supervisor to use FINDER?		
	Frequency	Percent
No	352	87.6%
Yes	46	11.4%
No answer	4	1.0%
Total	402	100.0%

18. Has your job changed since you began using FINDER?

	Frequency	Percent
No	311	78.7%
Yes	84	21.3%
Total	395	100.0%

19. How often do you use FINDER?

	Frequency	Percent
Almost never	91	22.9%
Few times a month	122	30.7%
About once a week	37	9.3%
Few times a week	68	17.1%
Almost every day	80	20.1%
Total	398	100.0%

20. What kind of FINDER training have you received?

	Frequency	Percent
Co-worker or supervisor, UCF, and agency training	3	0.8%
Co-worker or supervisor and UCF training	10	2.5%
Co-worker or supervisor and agency training	10	2.5%
Agency training and UCF training	7	1.8%
Co-worker or supervisor training only	150	38.1%
UCF training only	35	8.9%
Agency training only	56	14.2%
No training	123	31.2%
Total	394	100.0%

Appendix A (continued)

	Question		SD	MD	D	Neither	A	MA	SA
21	FINDER helps me do my job more efficiently. N=356	Freq.	3	0	6	53	123	36	135
		%	0.8%	0%	1.7%	14.9%	34.6%	10.1%	37.9%
22	FINDER is easy to use. N=374	Freq.	3	1	5	31	116	73	145
		%	0.8%	0.3%	1.3%	8.3%	31.0%	19.5%	38.8%
23	I use FINDER only as a last resort. N=354	Freq.	2	7	16	53	129	23	124
		%	35.0%	6.5%	36.4%	15.0%	4.5%	2.0%	0.6%
24	I use FINDER to locate missing or stolen property. N=305	Freq.	12	2	17	45	92	18	119
		%	3.9%	0.7%	5.6%	14.8%	30.2%	5.9%	39.0%
25	I use FINDER to locate information about people. N=360	Freq.	3	2	10	36	108	48	153
		%	0.8%	0.6%	2.8%	10.0%	30.0%	13.3%	42.5%

Appendix A (continued)

	Question		SD	MD	D	Neither	A	MA	SA
26	I am usually comfortable with learning new computer programs. N=379	Freq.	6	1	10	28	94	74	166
		%	1.6%	0.3%	2.6%	7.4%	24.8%	19.5%	43.8%
27	FINDER provides me information that I cannot get from any other source. N=361	Freq.	4	3	22	77	85	74	96
		%	1.1%	0.8%	6.1%	21.3%	23.5%	20.5%	26.6%
28	FINDER has helped me improve my job performance. N=355	Freq.	4	1	14	82	105	71	78
		%	1.1%	0.3%	3.9%	23.1%	29.6%	20.0%	22.0%
29	FINDER has helped me locate people that I couldn't find through other techniques. N=349	Freq.	7	3	28	110	91	47	63
		%	2.0%	0.9%	8.0%	31.5%	26.1%	13.5%	18.1%
30	I use FINDER to search for property more than I use it to search for people. N=338	Freq.	29	6	62	81	63	31	66
		%	8.6%	1.8%	18.3%	24.0%	18.6%	9.2%	19.5%

Appendix A (continued)

			SD	MD	D	Neither	A	MA	SA
31	In my job I have to use multiple computer systems to assemble the information I need. N=376	Freq.	10	3	30	29	124	45	135
		%	2.7%	0.8%	8.0%	7.7%	33.0%	12.0%	35.9%
32	My co-workers often ask me to help them with computer problems. N=368	Freq.	10	7	44	64	113	46	84
		%	2.7%	1.9%	12.0%	17.4%	30.7%	12.5%	22.8%
33	Most of the time, FINDER provides information that is useful to me. N=362	Freq.	2	3	8	58	130	75	86
		%	0.6%	0.8%	2.2%	16.0%	35.9%	20.7%	23.8%
34	I only use FINDER if I am looking for a person or property outside of my jurisdiction. N=357	Freq.	64	18	120	52	53	24	26
		%	17.9%	5.0%	33.6%	14.6%	14.8%	6.7%	7.3%
35	I use FINDER's "Link Analysis" to get the information I need. N=309	Freq.	9	6	49	112	80	27	26
		%	2.9%	1.9%	15.9%	36.2%	25.9%	8.7%	8.4%

Appendix A (continued)

	Question		SD	MD	D	Neither	A	MA	SA
36	FINDER has helped me solve or prevent crimes. N=306	Freq.	9	4	29	89	64	47	64
		%	2.9%	1.3%	9.5%	29.1%	20.9%	15.4%	20.9%
37	I have to make a lot of queries on FINDER to get the information I need. N=350	Freq.	10	13	60	102	111	27	27
		%	2.9%	3.7%	17.1%	29.1%	31.7%	7.7%	7.7%
38	I work with someone who is always encouraging me to use FINDER. N=329	Freq.	35	12	77	111	59	14	21
		%	10.6%	3.6%	23.4%	33.7%	17.9%	4.3%	6.4%
39	My co-workers often ask me to help them how to use FINDER software. N=353	Freq.	19	13	59	87	91	27	57
		%	5.4%	3.7%	16.7%	24.6%	25.8%	7.6%	16.1%
40	I would use FINDER more often if it did not take so long to get a response to my queries. N=354	Freq.	21	17	47	111	106	11	41
		%	5.9%	4.8%	13.3%	31.4%	29.9%	3.1%	11.6%
41	My job requires me to do a lot of data analysis. N=364	Freq.	26	8	60	93	97	26	54
		%	7.1%	2.2%	16.5%	25.5%	26.6%	7.1%	14.8%

Appendix A (continued)

Question		SD	MD	D	Neither	A	MA	SA
42 FINDER saves me a lot of time. N=357	Freq	5	3	22	125	106	45	51
	%	1.4%	0.8%	6.2%	35.0%	29.7%	12.6%	14.3%
43 I think FINDER is poorly designed. N=364	Freq.	2	2	8	83	146	47	76
	%	20.9%	12.9%	40.1%	22.8%	2.2%	0.5%	0.5%
44 I have computer tools other than FINDER to help me get information from outside of my jurisdiction. N=370	Freq.	47	36	137	58	49	20	23
	%	6.2%	5.4%	13.2%	15.7%	37.0%	9.7%	12.7%
45 It is easy for me to give specific examples of how FINDER has helped me do my job. N=346	Freq.	8	7	34	103	117	38	39
	%	2.3%	2.0%	9.8%	29.8%	33.8%	11.0%	11.3%
46 I could get better results from FINDER if I were provided more training about how to use it. N=361	Freq.	22	19	75	112	83	18	32
	%	6.1%	5.3%	20.8%	31.0%	23.0%	5.0%	8.9%

Appendix A (continued)

	Question		SD	MD	D	Neither	A	MA	SA
47	FINDER would be more useful to me if it had analytical tools. N=349	Freq.	17	18	73	159	55	16	11
		%	3.2%	4.6%	15.8%	45.6%	20.9%	5.2%	4.9%
48	The best thing about FINDER is I can get information that I was not able to get before. N=359	Freq.	2	4	8	67	133	62	83
		%	0.6%	1.1%	2.2%	18.7%	37.0%	17.3%	23.1%
49	FINDER is the only computer tool I have to get information from other police agencies. N=369	Freq.	47	22	122	56	62	23	37
		%	12.7%	6.0%	33.1%	15.2%	16.8%	6.2%	10.0%

Appendix A (continued)

50. Which of the following best represents the workload measure that you use in your job?		
	Frequency	Percent
Number of calls	42	10.5
Number of cases	211	52.9
Number of projects	60	15.0
Number of reports	3	0.8
Number of people met	7	1.8
None of the above	76	19.0
Total	399	100.0

51. In your current job assignment, do you maintain some measure, statistic, or record of your workload?		
	Frequency	Percent
No	70	17.5
Yes	330	82.5
Total	400	100.0

52. On average, how many [calls, cases, projects, meetings] do you handle each month?		
	Frequency	Percent
Fewer than 10	28	8.5
Between 10 and 50	185	56.1
Between 51 and 100	76	23.0
More than 100	41	12.4
Total	330	100.0

APPENDIX B: RELATIONSHIPS OF INSTRUMENT ITEMS
TO STUDY VARIABLES

Variable	Items	Description/Comments
User-level Success	1-7	Level of success (specific policing outcomes)
	21	User efficiency
	28	Change in performance
	36	Level of success (solving or preventing crimes)
	42	User efficiency
	45	User has examples of success
FINDER Task-fit	22	Ease of use
	24,30	Useful data, property
	25	Useful data, people
	27	Useful data, locatability, level of detail
	29,48	Useful data, not previously available Useful data, most of time
	33	Useful data outside jurisdiction
	34	Useful data, link analysis
	35	Ease of use
	37	Usability (negative) too long of time
	40	Routine/non-routine, multiple systems
	43	Usability (negative)
	47	Usability (negative) analytical tools
Computer Expertise	26	Computer expertise, new software
	32	Computer literacy, assisting others
	39	Computer literacy, assisting others
Usage Rate	19	Users' recall of usage rate
Job Assignment	11	Sworn or non-sworn
	12	Job function
	13	Job rank
	14	Job title
	18	Control for changes in job assignment.
	41	Routine/non-routine tasks

APPENDIX C: STATISTICAL TESTS & CONVENTIONS

Statistical Test	Data Type	Comments	Sources
Cramer's V ("phi")	Nominal	Chi-square based	Aldridge, 2001; Norusis, 2005
gamma	Ordinal	Asymmetric associations (directional)	Babbie, 1995; Weisberg et al, 1996
Independent Samples t-Test	Scale	Comparison of means between two independent samples	Gliner & Morgan, 2000; Kachigan, 1986; Norusis, 2005
Kendall's tau ("tau")	Ordinal	Symmetric associations tau-b for 2x2 comparisons; tau-c for others	Weisberg et al, 1996; Norusis, 2005
lambda	Nominal	PRE-based	Norusis, 2005; Gliner & Morgan, 2000
Levene Test for Homogeniety of Variance	Scale	Checks for equal variance between samples for ANOVA	Norusis, 2005
Mann-Whitney	Ordinal	Comparison of means for two-sample, unpaired data	Gliner & Morgan, 2000; Liao, 2002
Multiple Regression	Scale & dichotomous	Predictive relationship of multiple Variables on single outcome variable (single path)	Gliner & Morgan, 2000; Kachigan, 1986; Norusis, 2005
One-way ANOVA	Scale	Comparison of means between three or more groups	Norusis, 2005; Gliner & Morgan, 2000
Pearson Product-moment coefficient	Scale	Bivariate correlation	Babbie, 1995; Gliner & Morgan, 2000; Norusis, 2005
Spearman's rho ("rho")	Ordinal & non-normal scale	Association where both variables rank ordered	Weisberg et al, 1996; Aldridge, 2001; Norusis, 2005
Structural equation modeling	Scale & dichotomous	Simultaneous predictive relation-ship of multiple variables on one or more outcomes	Kline, 2005; Maruyama, 1998; Wan, 2002

Convention Used for Interpreting Correlation Coefficient (Losh,2002)	
Correlation Value	Verbal Designation
0.0	No relationship
0.1 to .10	Very Weak
.11 to .25	Weak
.26 to .50	Moderate
.51 to .75	Strong
.76 to .99	Very Strong
1.00	Perfect association

Convention Used for Cramer's V Statistic
(Standard Table & Graph Format & Interpretation, 2004)

Cramer's V Statistic	Verbal Designation
Less than .10	Weak
.10 to .29	Moderate
.30 or higher	Strong

Convention Used for lambda Statistic
(Schwab, 2004)

lambda Statistic	Verbal Designation
0.0	No relationship
0.0 to 0.2	Very weak
0.2 to 0.4	Weak
0.4 to 0.6	Moderate
0.6 to 0.8	Strong
0.8 to 1.0	Very strong
1.0	Perfect relationship

APPENDIX D: CORRELATION COEFFICIENTS (r)
IN PRIOR RESEARCH

Author(s)	Description	Approximate r value *
Goodhue (1995)	Used Task-technology fit (TTF) instrument with 259 technology users in 9 companies. Significant variables related to system usefulness & usability related to user tasks ranged from adj r-square .11 to .30	.33-.55
Colvin & Goh (2005)	Used Technology Acceptance Measure (TAM) with 430 patrol officers in one city. r-squared =.22 for ease of use and .22 for usability of technology systems.	.47
Dishaw & Strong (1999)	Used combination of TTF and TAM instruments across 60 IT projects in 3 corporations. The combined effect of TTF and TAM was r-squared=.51	.71
Legris et al (2003)	Reviewed use of TAM across multiple research domains and concluded that TAM consistently predicts about 40% of system use.	.63
Davis (1989)	Developed TAM and tested across organizations in 3 studies (combined n=300). r values from .45 to .85	.45-.85
Danziger & Kraemer (1985)	Studied 374 detectives in 40 agencies & influence of technology on performance. r values of influence of IT on performance ranged from .34-.56	.34-.56
Venkatesh & Davis (2000)	Extended TAM to TAM II and tested longitudinally across 4 systems and 156 users with sub-groups of voluntary and mandatory users. In the voluntary use group, r-square across 3 time period ranged from .44-.60	.66-.77
Goodhue & Thompson (1995)	Used TTF instrument on 600 users in 2 companies. Adjusted r-square across relevant TTF dimensions ranged from .10 to .25	.32-.50

REFERENCES

Ackoff, R. L. (1989). From data to wisdom. *Journal of Applied Systems Analysis*, 16, 3-9.

Aldridge, A. & Levine, K. (2001). *Surveying the social world: Principles and practice in survey research.* Philadelphia, PA: Open University Press.

Alreck, P.L. & Settle, R.B. (1995) *The Survey research handbook* (2nd ed.) Chicago: Irwin.

Babbie, E. (1995). *The practice of social research* (7th ed.). New York: Wadsworth Publishing Company.

Bazan, E. B. (2007). *The Foreign Intelligence Surveillance Act: A brief overview of selected issues.* Congressional Research Service, Order Code RL34279. Retrieved January 2, 2008 from: http://www.fas.org/sgp/crs/intel/RL34279.pdf.

Better warrant system needed. (2001, October 24). *South Florida Sun – Sentinel*, p. 30.A.

Bharati, P. and Chaudhury, A. (2004). An empirical investigation of decision-making satisfaction in web-based decision support systems. *Decision Support Systems, 37*, 187-197.

Brantingham, P., & Brantingham, P. (1984). *Patterns in crime.* New York: Macmillan Publishing Company.

Bureau of Justice Assistance. (2002). *Mission possible: Strong governance structures for the integration of justice information systems.* Retrieved October 18, 2005 from: http://www.ncjrs.org/pdffiles1/bja/192278.pdf.

Bureau of Justice Assistance [BJA] Center for Program Evaluation (June 6, 2005). *Information sharing/integration Initiatives.* Retrieved November 3, 2005 from: http://www.ojp.usdoj.gov/BJA/evaluation/psi_isii/index.htm.

Bureau of Justice Statistics [BJS] (1997). *Implementing the national incident-based reporting system: A project status report.* NCJ-165581, Retrieved May 24, 2008 from:
http://www.ojp.usdoj.gov/bjs/pub/pdf/inibrs.pdf.

Bureau of Justice Statistics [BJS] Justice Statistics Improvement Program (July 15, 2005). *National Incident-Based Reporting System (NIBRS) Implementation Program.* Retrieved May 24, 2008 from:
http://www.ojp.usdoj.gov/bjs/nibrs.htm#F&A.

Burton, S. E., Finn, M., Livingston, D., Padgett, K, and Scully, K. (2002). *Typology of inter-jurisdictional offenders in Florida.* Retrieved June 3, 2005 from the Florida Department of Law Enforcement, Florida Statistical Analysis Center Web site:
http://www.fdle.state.fl.us/fsac/Publications/mobility_report.pdf.

Bush, G. W. (2002). *The Department of Homeland Security.* Retrieved January 2, 2008 from http://www.dhs.gov/xlibrary/assets/book.pdf.

Bush, G. W. (2007). *National strategy for information sharing: Successes and challenges in improving terrorism-related information sharing.* White House: author.

Carter, David, L. (2004). *Law enforcement intelligence: A guide for state, local, and tribal law enforcement agencies.* Washington, D.C.: U.S. Department of Justice Office of Community Oriented Policing Services.

Center for Law Enforcement Technology, Training, & Research, Inc. [LETTR] (2008). *About the Law Enforcement Data Sharing Consortium & FINDER.* Retrieved May 2, 2008 from:
http://www.lettr.org/FINDER/tabid/76/Default.aspx.

Chen, H., Schroeder, J., Hauck, R. V., Ridgeway, L., Atabakhsh, H., Gupta, H., et al. (2002). COPLINK connect: Information and knowledge management for law enforcement. *Decision Support Systems, 34,* 271-285.

Cohen, J. (1977). *Statistical power analysis for the behavioral sciences* (Rev. ed.). New York: Academic Press.

Cohen, J. (1988). *Statistical power analysis for the behavioral science.* (2nd ed.). Hillsdale, NJ: Lawrence Erlbaum Associates.

Colvin, C. A. and Goh, A. (2005). Validation of the technology acceptance model for police. *Journal of Criminal Justice, 33,* 89-95.

Commission on Accreditation of Law Enforcement Agencies [CALEA] (1998). *Standards for law enforcement agencies* (4th Edition with revisions through 2000). Fairfax, VA.: author.

Cox III, E. P. (1980). The optimal number of response alternatives for a scale: A review. *Journal of Marketing Research, 17,* 407-422.

Danziger, J. N. and Kraemer, K. L. (1985 Jan/Feb). Computerized data-based systems and productivity among professional workers: The case of detectives. *Public Administration Review,* 196-209.

Davis, F. (1989). Perceived usefulness, perceived ease of use, and user acceptance of information technology. *MIS Quarterly,* 13, 319-340.

Dillman, D. A. (2000). *Mail and Internet surveys: The Tailored Design Method.* New York: John Wiley and Sons, Inc.

Dishaw, M. T. & Strong, D. M. (1999). Extending the technology acceptance model with task-technology fit constructs. *Information & Management, 36,* 9-21.

Dunworth, T. (2001). Criminal justice and the IT revolution. *Criminal Justice 2000, Volume 3,* National Institute of Justice. [Electronic version]. Retrieved September 13, 2003, from: http://www.ncjrs.org/criminal_justice2000/vol_3/03h.pdf.

Faggiani, D. and McLaughlin, C. (1999). Using National Incident-Based Reporting System data for strategic crime analysis. *Journal of Quantitative Criminology, 15* (2), 181-191.

Federal Bureau of Investigation [FBI] (2002). *An NCIC milestone.* Press release distributed March 23, 2002. Retrieved November 11, 2004 from http://www.fbi.gov/pressrel/pressrel02/ncic032302.htm.

Federal Bureau of Investigation [FBI] (2005a). CJIS Division homepage for National Crime Information Center. Retrieved November 13, 2005 from http://www.fbi.gov/hq/cjisd/ncic.htm.

Federal Bureau of Investigation [FBI] (2005b). *Passport information sharing with Department of State.* Written record of comments by Thomas E. Bush III, Assistant Director, Criminal Justice Information Services Division, FBI, before the Senate Committee on Homeland Security and Governmental Affairs on June 29, 2005. Retrieved November 13, 2005 from http://www.fbi.gov/congress/congress05.htm.

Federal Bureau of Investigation [FBI] (2007). National Incident-Based Reporting System (NIBRS). Retrieved May 2, 2008 from http://www.fbi.gov/ucr/faqs.htm.

Florida Department of Law Enforcement [FDLE] (April 15, 2005). Press release: Matrix Project Concludes. Retrieved May 22, 2006 from http://www.fdle.state.fl.us/press_releases/expired/2005/20050415-matrix_project.html.

Florida Department of Law Enforcement [FDLE] (March 1, 2005). "FT LE officers by Region." Excel data file provided to author detailing number of full-time sworn officers per Florida agency.

Florida Integrated Network for Data Exchange and Retrieval [FINDER] (2006). Computer application provided through the Florida Law Enforcement Data Sharing Consortium and the University of Central Florida. Restricted to law enforcement users.

Fyfe, J. J., Greene, J. R., Walsh, W. F., Wilson, O. W., & McLaren, R. C. (1997). *Police administration.* (5th Edition). New York: McGraw Hill.

Gliem, J. A. & Gliem, R. R. (2003, October). *Calculating, interpreting, and reporting Cronbach's Alpha Reliability Coefficient for Likert-type scales.* Paper presented at the Midwest Research-to-Practice Conference in Adult, Continuing, and Community Education, The Ohio State University, Columbus, OH, October 8-10, 2003.

Gliner, J. A. & Morgan, G.A. (2000). *Research methods in applied settings*. Mahwah, NJ: Lawrence Erlbaum Associates.

Global Justice Information Sharing Initiative (2004). *National criminal intelligence sharing plan*. U.S. Department of Justice, Office of Justice Programs. Retrieved January 2, 2008 from: http://it.ojp.gov/documents/NCISP_Plan.pdf.

Global Justice Information Sharing Initiative (2005). *Executive summary: National criminal intelligence sharing plan.* U.S. Department of Justice, Office of Justice Programs. Retrieved January 2, 2008 from:
http://it.ojp.gov/documents/NCISP_executive_summary.pdf.

Global Justice Information Sharing Initiative (n.d.). *Fusion center guidelines: Developing and sharing information and intelligence in a new era.* U.S. Department of Justice, Office of Justice Programs. Retrieved January 2, 2008 from:
http://it.ojp.gov/documents/fusion_center_guidelines.pdf.

Goodhue, D. L. (1995). Understanding user evaluations of information systems. *Management Sciences, 41*, 1827-1844.

Goodhue, D. L. (1998). Development and measurement validity of a task-technology fit instrument for user evaluations of information systems. *Decision Sciences, 29* (1), 105- 138.

Goodhue, D. L. & Thompson, R. L. (1995,). Task-technology fit and individual performance. *MIS Quarterly, 19*, 213-236.

Government Accountability Office (2006). *Information sharing: DHS should take steps to encourage more widespread use of its programs to protect and share critical infrastructure information.* [GAO Publication No. GAO-06-383.] Retrieved May 23, 2006 from:
http://www.gao.gov/new.items/d06383.pdf.

Government Accountability Office (2003). *Homeland security: Information sharing responsibilities, challenges, and key management issues.* [GAO Publication No. GAO-03-1165T] Retrieved January 3, 2008 from http://www.gao.gov/new.items/d031165t.pdf.

Gujarati, D. N. (2003). *Basic econometrics* (4th ed.). New York: McGraw Hill.

Hair, J.F., Anderson, R. E., Tatham, R. L., & Black, W. C. (1998). *Multivariate data analysis* (5th ed.). New York: Prentice-Hall

Hauck, R. V., Atabakhsh, H., Ongvasith, P., Gupta, H., & Chen, H. (2001). *COPLINK concept space: An application for criminal intelligence analysis.* Tucson, AZ: University of Arizona, Department of Management Information Systems.

Hasson, D. & Arnetz, B. B. (2005). Validation and findings comparing VAS vs. Likert scales for psychosocial measurements. *International Electronic Journal of Health Education,* 8, 178-192.

Hinduja, S. (2004). Perceptions of local and state law enforcement concerning the role of computer crime investigative teams. *Policing: An International Journal of Police Strategies & Management, 27* (3), 341-357.

Hurley, A. E., Scandura, T. A., Schriesheim, C. A., Brannick, M. T., Seers, A., Vandenber, R. J. & Williams, L. J. (1997). Exploratory and confirmatory factor analyses: guidelines, issues and alternatives. *Journal of Organizational Behavior, 18,* 667-683.

Intelligence Reform and Terrorism Prevention Act of 2004 [Terrorism Act of 2004]. (December 7, 2004) [online version]   Retrieved November 12, 2004 from: http://govtaff.senate.gov/_files/IntelligenceReformconferencereportlegi slativelanguage12704.pdf.

Ioimo, R. E. (2000). *Applying the theory of task technology fit in assessing police use of field mobile computing.* (Unpublished doctoral dissertation, Nova Southeastern University, Buffalo, FL)   UMI# 9988001. Available at http://wwwlib.umi.com.

Ioimo, R. E. & Aronson, J. E. (2003). The benefits of police field mobile computing realized by non-patrol sections of a police department. *International Journal of Police Science & Management, 5* (3), 195-206.

Kachigan, S. K. (1986). *Multivariate statistical analysis*. New York: Radius Press.

Kim, C.S. & Keith, N.K. (1994). Computer literacy topics: A comparison of views within a business school. *Journal of Information Systems Education*, Summer, 6 (2), 55-57.

Kline, R. B. (2005). *Principles and Practice of Structural Equation Modeling* (2nd Edition). New York: Guilford Press.

Kraemer, H. C. & Thiemann, S. (1987). *How many subjects?* Newbury Park, CA: Sage Publications.

Legris, P., Ingham, J. & Collerette, P. (2003). Why do people use information technology? A critical review of the technology acceptance model. *Information & Management, 40,* 191-204.

Liao, T. F. (2002). *Statistical group comparison*. New York: Wiley-Interscience.

Lin, C. (2004). Examining technology usability and acceptance in digital government: A case study in law enforcement. (Doctoral dissertation, University of Arizona, 2004). *Dissertation Abstracts International, 65/04,* 1446.

Lipowicz, A. (5 October, 2005). *Schism downs JRIES homeland security network.* WashingtonTechnology.com. Retrieved May 2, 2008 from:
http://www.washingtontechnology.com/online/1_1/27115-1.html.

Long, E. & Franklin, A.L. (2004). The paradox of implementing the Government Performance and Results Act: Top-down direction for bottom-up implementation. *Public Administration Review, 64,* 309-319.

Losh, S. C. (2002). *Guide 5: Bivariate associations and correlation coefficient properties.* Retrieved April 6, 2006 from Florida State University, Department of Educational Psychology and Learning Systems Web site: http://edf5400-01.sp02.fsu.edu/Guide5.html.

Markle Foundation (2003). *Creating a trusted network for homeland security.* Retrieved January 2, 2008 from: http://www.markletaskforce.org/Report2_Full_Report.pdf.

Maruyama, G. M. (1998). *Basics of Structural Equation Modeling.* Thousand Oaks, CA: Sage Publications Inc.

McGroddy, J. C. & Lin, H.S. (editors) (2004). *A Review of FBI's Trilogy Information Technology Modernization Program.* Washington: National Academies Press.

McMillan, J. H. & Schumacher, S. (1993*). Research in education* (3rd ed.). New York: Harper Collins College Publishers.

Mitretek Corporation (2005, October 7) *Comprehensive Regional Information Sharing Project (CRISP).* Retrieved February 13, 2006 from http://www.cshs-us.org/home.nsf/CriminalJustice/current#crisp.

Moore, T. (2001, June 11). FDLE policy on gun database is limited by law. *St. Petersburg Times.* Retrieved September 18, 2006 from: http://www.sptimes.com/News/061101/Opinion/FDLE_policy_on_gun _da.shtml.

National Commission on Terrorist Attacks [9/11 Commission] (2004). *The 9/11 Commission Report: Final Report of the National Commission on Terrorist Attacks Upon the United States.* New York: W.W. Norton.

National Governors Association [NGA] (2002). *Improving public safety through justice information sharing.* Retrieved October 27, 2003, from the National Governors Association Web site: http://www.nga.org/cda/files/JUSTICEINTEGRATIONIB.pdf.

Noblis (2006). *Comprehensive regional information-sharing project volume 1: Metrics for the evaluation of law enforcement information-sharing systems.* Noblis Technical Report MTR-2006-035 prepared for U.S. Department of Justice under award 2001-LT-BX-K002. Retrieved March 26, 2008 from: http://www.ncjrs.gov/pdffiles1/nij/grants/219377.pdf.Norusis, M. J. (2005).

Norusis, M. J. (2005). *SPSS 13.0 statistical procedures companion.* Upper Saddle River, NJ: Prentice-Hall.

Nunn, S. (2001). Police information technology: Assessing the effects of computerization on urban police functions. *Public Administration Review, 61,* 221-234.

Nunn, S. & Quinet, K. (2002). Evaluating the effects of information technology on problem-oriented-policing. *Evaluation Review, 26* (1), 81-108.

Office of Homeland Security (2002, July). *National strategy for homeland security.* Retrieved September 19, 2003 from: http://www.whitehouse.gov/homeland/book/nat_strat_hls.pdf.

Peterson, M. (2005). *Intelligence-led policing: The new intelligence architecture.* Bureau of Justice Assistance, Office of Justice Programs, NCJ # 210681. Retrieved January 4, 2008 from: http://www.ncjrs.gov/pdffiles1/bja/210681.pdf.

Rengert, G. F., Piquero, A. R., & Jones, P. R. (1999, May). Distance decay reexamined. *Criminology, 37*(2), 427-445.

Reynolds, K. M., Griset, P. L., & Eaglin, R. (2005). Controlling terrorism through automated sharing of low-level law enforcement data. *Law Enforcement Executive Forum, 5* (6), 127-135.

Reynolds, K. M., Griset, P., & Scott Jr., E. D. (2006). Law enforcement information sharing: A Florida case study." *American Journal of Criminal Justice, 31,* 1-18.

Schwab, J. (2004). *Social work statistics class notes.* Retrieved April 7, 2006 from the University of Texas at Austin, School of Social Work Web site: http://www.utexas.edu/courses/schwab/sw318_spring_2004/SolvingProblems/Class11_LambdaNGamma.ppt.

Scott Jr., E. D. (2004). Unpublished research. Orange County Sheriff's Office, Orlando, FL.

Scott Jr., E. D. (2005). Unpublished research. University of Central Florida, College of Health & Public Affairs, Department of Criminal Justice & Legal Studies.

Senese, J. D. (1997). *Applied research methods in criminal justice.* Chicago: Nelson-Hall.

Smith, B., Caputi,, P. & Rawstorne, P. (2000). Differentiating computer experience and attitudes toward computers: an empirical investigation. *Computers in Human Behavior, 16,* 59-81.

Smith, J. (2004). Strengthening crime data reporting at the Broward Sheriff's Office. A report By Independent Counsel Jim Smith, Esq.and the Collins Center for Public Policy, Inc. Retrieved May 2, 2008 from the Collins Center website at:
http://www.collinscenter.org/usr_doc/BSO_Final_Report.pdf.

Sprent, P. & Smeeton, N. C. (2001). *Applied nonparametric statistical methods.* New York: Chapman & Hall/CRC.

SPSS, Inc. (2005). Statistical Graduate Pack 13.5 (software).

Standard table and graph format and interpretation. (2004). Retrieved April 6, 2006 from Rutgers, State University of New Jersey, Department of Sociology, Anthropology and Criminal Justice Web site: http://sociology.camden.rutgers.edu/curriculum/format.htm.

Thompson, B. (2005). *Exploratory and confirmatory factor analysis.* Washington DC: American Psychological Association.

U.S. Census Bureau (2005). Florida population by county. Retrieved May 23, 2008 from http://factfinder.census.gov/servlet/
GCTTable?_bm=n&_lang=en&mt_name=DEC_2000_PL_U_GCTPL_
ST2&format=ST2&_box_head_nbr=GCTPL&ds_name=DEC_2000_P
L_U&geo_id=04000US12.

U.S. Department of Defense (2002, May 22). News Transcript: *Secretary Rumsfeld media availability.* Retrieved January 2, 2008 from: http://www.defenselink.mil/transcripts/transcript.aspx?transcriptid=345
7.

U.S. Department of Energy (1995). *How to measure performance: A handbook of techniques and tools*. Retrieved February 8, 2006 from: http://www.orau.gov/pbm/documents/handbook1a.html.

U.S. Department of Justice (2002, October 9). Attorney General John Ashcroft unveils Gateway Information Sharing Pilot Project in St. Louis, Missouri. Press Release 02-589. Retrieved September 19, 2006 from http://www.usdoj.gov/opa/pr/2002/October/02_ag_589.htm.

U.S. Department of Justice, Office of Justice Programs, Bureau of Justice Statistics (2003, August). Survey of State Criminal History Information Systems, 2001 A Criminal Justice Information Policy Report. NCJ 200343 Retrieved March 22, 2006 from: http://www.ojp.usdoj.gov/bjs/pub/pdf/sschis01.pdf.

U.S. Department of Justice [DOJ] (April 2004). *The National Criminal Intelligence Sharing Plan.* [online version] Retrieved March 23, 2005 from: http://it.ojp.gov/documents/National_Criminal_Intelligence_Sharing-Plan.pdf. [Note: Earlier versions (1.0) of this plan were published online in October 2003].

U.S. Department of Justice, Office of Justice Programs, Information Technology Initiatives, (n.d.). Global Justice XML Model. Retrieved February 13, 2006 from: http://it.ojp.gov/topic.jsp?topic_id=43.

United States Government Accountability Office (2006a). *Information sharing: The federal government needs to establish policies and processes for sharing terrorism-related and sensitive but unclassified information.* [GAO Publication No. GAO-06-385]. Washington, DC. Retrieved May 23, 2006 from: http://www.gao.gov/new.items/d06385.pdf.

U.S. House Committee on Homeland Security Democratic Staff (2006). *Leaving the nation at risk: 33 unfulfilled promises from the Department of Homeland Security.* Retrieved May 22, 2006 from: http://hsc-democrats.house.gov/NR/rdonlyres/1C607310-3228-4CCC-B13A04A808A4C19B/0/HomelandSecurityDemocratsRevealUnfulfilledPromises.pdf.

van Belle, G. (2002) *Statistical rules of thumb.* New York: Wiley-Interscience.

Venkatesh, V. and Davis, F. D. (2000). A theoretical extension of the Technology Acceptance Model: Four longitudinal field studies. *Management Science, 46* (2), 186–204.

Venkatesh, V., Morris, M. G., Davis, G. B., & Davis, F. D. (2003). User acceptance of information technology: Toward a unified view. *MIS Quarterly, 27* 425-478.

Wan, T. T. H. (2002). *Evidence-based health care management.* Norwell, MA: Kluwer Academic Publishers.

Weisberg, H. F., Krosnick, J. A., & Bowen, B. D. (1996). *An introduction to survey research, polling, and data analysis.* Thousand Oaks, CA: Sage.

Witzig, E. W. (2003). The new ViCAP: More user-friendly and used by more agencies. *FBI Law Enforcement Bulletin, 72* (6), 1-7.

Zaworski, M. J. (2004). Assessing an automated, information-sharing technology in the post '9-11' era: Do local law enforcement officers think it meets their needs? (Doctoral dissertation, Florida Atlantic University, 2004). *Dissertation Abstracts International, 65/04,* 1536.

INDEX